Rimbaud

Rimbaud
The Cost of Genius

Neal Oxenhandler

THE OHIO STATE UNIVERSITY PRESS | COLUMBUS

Copyright © 2009 by The Ohio State University.
All rights reserved

Library of Congress Cataloging-in-Publication Data
Oxenhandler, Neal.
  Rimbaud : the cost of genius / Neal Oxenhandler.
     p. cm.
  Includes bibliographical references and index.
  ISBN-13: 978-0-8142-1054-3 (cloth : alk. paper)
  ISBN-10: 0-8142-1054-6 (cloth : alk. paper)
  1. Rimbaud, Arthur, 1854–1891—Psychology. 2. Rimbaud, Arthur, 1854–1891—Criticism and interpretation. I. Title.
  PQ2387.R5Z747 2009
  841'.8—dc22
                                        2008043022

This book is available in the following editions:
Cloth (ISBN 978-08142-1054-3)
CD-ROM (ISBN 978-08142-9192-4)
Paper (ISBN: 978-0-8142-5674-9)
Cover design by DesignSmith
Text design by Juliet Williams
Type set in Adobe Sabon

For my children
Noelle, Daniel, and Alicia

Do we hear with sufficient clarity, in the poetic discourse of Arthur Rimbaud, the part of silence? And do we begin to find there the horizon that he attained?

—Martin Heidegger

Contents

Acknowledgments   xi

Introduction   1

PART I. "HIS DAY!"

Chapter 1   Overview: Rimbaud and Psychocriticism   11

PART II. "HE IS AFFECTION AND THE PRESENT"

Chapter 2   Defiance in "Les Poètes de sept ans"   19
Chapter 3   Poem of the Uncanny: "Le Bateau ivre"   24
Chapter 4   Figures of Desire in "Mémoire"   33

PART III. "IT IS THIS PRESENT AGE THAT HAS FAILED!"

Chapter 5   What Happened in Babylone?
              "Le Coeur du pitre"; Survival of the Object in
              "Qu'est-ce pour nous, mon coeur . . . ?"   43
Chapter 6   Synchronicity: "A Une Raison"; "Démocratie"   51

PART IV. " . . . THE MOST INTENSE MUSIC"

Chapter 7   The Child as Thaumaturge: "Après le déluge"   59
Chapter 8   Abreaction in Three Poems: "Honte"; "Angoisse"; "Aube"   65
Chapter 9   Fantasy and Reality: "Vies I, II, III"; "H"   75
Chapter 10   Killing Me Softly: "Conte"   82
Chapter 11   "Nocturne vulgaire" and the Paranoid Position   88

PART V. "O FECUNDITY OF THE MIND AND IMMENSITY OF THE UNIVERSE!"
Chapter 12 "Génie": Advent of the Ego-Ideal   95
Chapter 13 Narcissistic Gain in "Solde"   103

PART VI. "HIS VISION, HIS VISION!"
Chapter 14 Rimbaud's Ontology: "Villes II"   111
Chapter 15 Sublimation in *Une Saison en enfer*   119

Appendix   The Death of Rimbaud: "We remember him and he travels on."   141

Notes   149
Bibliography   161
Index   167

Acknowledgments

Warmest thanks to Robert W. Greene, who was the first to read the manuscript and to perceive in this book a new vision of Rimbaud. Thanks also to James Lawler, president of "Les Amis de Rimbaud," who gave support and encouragement during the writing of *The Cost of Genius*. Paol Keineg read the text and the translations with a poet's precision. I thank my Dartmouth colleague, Lawrence D. Kritzman, who helped me work out the poetics of psychoanalysis, an important feature of the book. For the sections on Heidegger I express gratitude to the memory of my friend and former colleague at U.C. Santa Cruz, Albert Hofstadter, recalling equally our conversations and his wonderful translations. The book took shape at New College of Florida, where then provost, Charlene Callahan, generously gave me access to Cook Library. I wish also to praise two outstanding librarians at New College. Reference librarian Caroline Reed gave expert help at every stage of the book's development. Barbara Dubreuil of Interlibrary Loan provided a steady flow of documentation from the vast Rimbaud bibliography.

The cover image of Rimbaud, painted by his sometimes roommate Jean-Louis Forain (nicknamed Gavroche/le gamin de Paris), done in 1872 when Rimbaud was eighteen, and currently in a private collection, appears here by courtesy of the owner and of Jean-Jacques Lefrère.

Introduction

Arthur Rimbaud, the adolescent who revolutionized French poetry in the nineteenth century, was (even more than Baudelaire, whom he called "a true god") the creator of French literary modernism. Rimbaud has often been seen as unfathomable and his poetry as inaccessible. This was especially the case during the post-structuralist period (late sixties). Writing in *Tel Quel,* as a spokesman of structuralism ("the revolutionary textual science"), J. L. Baudry identifies in Rimbaud " . . . a scriptural practice which marks the struggle against the domination by meaning and expressivity." Baudry maintains that those who have interpreted Rimbaud are trying hopelessly to fill ". . . the hollow that this text seems to circumscribe or which is inherent in it. . . ."[1]

Like any human individual, Rimbaud was mysterious and contradictory; born with the hope and need to love, he was wet-nursed by Mme Cloutier, the wife of a nail-maker, under primitive conditions; his birth mother was a difficult person, unequal to her sensitive and gifted child. She herself had a painful childhood, losing her mother early and becoming a proxy wife and housekeeper to her father, whom she venerated. She lost her first daughter (who lived only three months), born after two boys, Frédéric and Arthur. Two more children, Vitalie and Isabelle, followed. Abandoned by Captain Frédéric Rimbaud, an army officer, after the birth of Isabelle, Mme Rimbaud was afflicted with a constitutional distrust of the petite bourgeoise society around her in Charleville, les Ardennes. She found her children a burden. Devoted though she was to her mother, Isabelle Rimbaud was overheard reproving her, "Quand on n'aime pas les enfants, on ne se marie pas."/ "If you don't like children, you shouldn't marry."[2] Arthur grew up a defiant teenager, both violent and tender. Even if Rimbaud seems at times more and less than a man, he must be accessible to the insights of what has come to be called, since Charles Mauron, psychocriticism.

My approach in this book is to provide original readings of major texts, with the aim of illuminating Rimbaud from within: what he feared and desired as man and poet in the age of Emperor Louis-Napoleon and (after the bloodbath of the Commune in October 1871) the Third Republic. In pursuing this goal I have at many points called on the resources of psychoanalysis. Each poem is also seen from the aesthetic standpoint. Its formal boundaries, its rhythmic patterns, its thematic resonances, its puzzles and ironies, are viewed in relation to a dominant psychic trope. I have tried to keep my readings open to theory, on the one hand, and to the "*envoûtement*" of a great poet, whose "spell" may sometimes be overpowering, on the other.

ALTHOUGH THE preferred approach to the poetry of Rimbaud continues to be aesthetic, Rimbaud's *oeuvre* remains a privileged nexus of psychoanalytic themes. What else have critics searched for but depth coherence, how else have they read his poetry except seeking to unveil the works' multiple enigmas?[3] Rimbaud's poems are, in Barthes's formula, "figures of desire," where psyche and text pursue each other, without one suppressing the other. Every text is invaded by fugitive imagos, like the drowned corpses that appear and disappear beside the drunken boat in "Le Bateau ivre." And how can we explain the critical fortunes of Rimbaud's work, rivaling the attention previously lavished on Racine and Pascal, except by the play of transference and countertransference in the continuing dialogue of his readers? We survivors and witnesses of "the Freud wars," as they have come to be called,[4] can never use psychoanalytic terms naively, reductively, for they too are figures of desire—dangerous in their polyvalence and ambiguity. Yet if they are not "scientific" as Freud vainly dreamed, they are validated by a century and a half of interaction through a network of seekers, who have given us a new and powerful revelation of the body–soul relation and a language to help us describe our findings in many fields. Because psychoanalysis uses language as its primary medium, it has a direct and powerful pertinence to literature.

THIS BOOK raises a fundamental question about Rimbaud, a question that arises in respect to any artist of his stature: what price did Rimbaud pay to realize his *oeuvre,* what is the cost of genius? And first, what are the proper conventions for dealing with genius? How is it possible to use psychoanalytic conventions, invented largely by medical doctors, to penetrate the secrets of a man who was one of the greatest literary figures of his century? Freud, of course, wrote about da Vinci; but then Freud was himself a genius. There is an imperative for each critic to consider the task anew: while this book calls on some of the major theorists of the psychoanalytic movement, I have been at pains to fashion their concepts to the specific case at hand.

As I have read and taught the poems of Rimbaud, I have become aware of a contract underlying each of them: for each poem, Rimbaud paid a price in suffering, in jealousy, in misunderstanding. He paid a price in the extreme difficulty of being Rimbaud. When you reinvent the literature of your time, you do so against the acquired inertia of that literature. It is like the second law of thermodynamics: to each act of poetic genius, there is an equal and opposite negation of that genius. A large part of the price Rimbaud paid for genius lay in the use he made of his own personality during the time he actively practiced *Voyance,* an ascetic discipline that gave rise to his visionary poetics. He was seventeen at the time he began this experiment. We tend to think of these two years as a time of exhibitionistic freedom; yet *Voyance* also involved repression and self-punishment. During Rimbaud's short career, his soaring ambition was constantly abraded by a reality that it was his destiny to change. He was at war with reality in all its conventional forms. During his career as a poet he never entirely abandoned *Voyance,* but allowed it to work itself out within him. It became a new and radical way of being in and knowing the world—an ontology.

And there is something else that cost him dearly: the way art steals from experience. This is one way to read "Angoisse," with its litany of failures and the burning regret for all he missed in life. The last paragraph spells out his bitter indemnity: wounds, torture, murder, and silence, worst of all.

This is a high price to pay for the privilege of genius and it was compounded by something even more acute: the originality of a poet who anticipated, by more than sixty years, the vision of Martin Heidegger. It is the great poets, Heidegger believed, who renew our history, who act as the guardians of being (*physis*), which, under the pressure of applied science (*techne*), periodically—and the 1870s was such a period—becomes rigid and inflexible. Throughout his entire work, but especially in the *Illumina-*

tions, Rimbaud reveals entities through a poetics that calls forth a world yet to come.[5] Not only was this poetics unfamiliar and suspect to many of his contemporaries; it was a frightening power to Rimbaud himself.

And the cost of genius kept climbing, until Rimbaud had no alternative except to abandon poetry and become the son his mother had always wanted—a merchant, intent on getting rich. He hoped to marry, settle down, become a *rentier,* have a son. Some years after his abandonment of poetry, in Africa, where he was toiling at a thankless job, he met a French traveler who asked him if he were indeed *"that* Rimbaud," recognized by the decadents as their *chef de file,* their forerunner and model. Rimbaud grimaced and said, "Je ne pense plus à ça!" ("I never think about that!") Had he written poetry? "Des rinçures." ("Dishwater.") Poetry, it seemed, had brought him nothing but humiliation and degradation.

While Rimbaud's poetry is intensely private, it is situated in a social context with which he interacted from a young age. The chaos of the historical period into which Rimbaud was born (the end of the Second Empire and the turmoil of the early years of the Third Republic) contributed to his *"désarroi"* or psychic stress. Some critics have tried to make him into "the poet of the Commune." Some of his poems about that tragic episode are powerful, others strident and immature. He was less the celebrant of the Commune than a frightened seventeen-year-old, marooned in a military barracks in Paris.

Rimbaud had a protected childhood but threw himself recklessly into the world, learning early how to endure hardship and to live among working-class men and women. Where did he really feel at home? From the time of his second escape to Paris (February–March 1871), when he walked all the way back to Charleville through the battle lines of the Franco-Prussian war, home was always his mother, the straight-backed, Jansenistic, blue-eyed Vitalie Veuve Rimbaud. (She began to call herself a widow after Captain Rimbaud's last departure, in September 1860, even though he was still very much alive, having retired from the army and moved to Dijon.)

THIS BOOK consists of six parts and an appendix. Part I reviews the present state of psychocritical study of Rimbaud. Part II examines three of Rimbaud's finest poems in regular verse form, "Les Poètes de sept ans," "Le Bateau ivre," and "Mémoire." "Les Poètes de sept ans" draws an unforgettable portrait of Rimbaud as a child, needy yet defiant. It is here that I first consider the attribution to Rimbaud (by Yves Bonnefoy) of a Nietzschean lineage. As the book progresses, the importance of Nietzsche diminishes in contrast to the foreshadowing of Heidegger, which becomes the philosophical focus of the book.

I have aligned "Le Bateau ivre" among those modern literary works (by Kafka, Proust, Borges) motivated by the uncanny.[6] "Mémoire" is read through the splitting of the family triad and the aggrandizing perception of a mother imago who swells to fill the entire Valley of the Meuse.[7]

Part III, chapter 5, begins with a reading of the poetic record ("Le Coeur du pitre") of what may have been an unwelcome sexual approach in the Babylone barracks of the National Guard during the Commune. Following this, also in chapter 5, is the paroxysmal text, "Qu'est-ce pour nous, mon coeur . . . ?," probably written during the *Semaine sanglante* (the Bloody Week) that terminated the Commune. Here I use D. W. Winnicott's way of asking if infantile aggression has been successfully negotiated. In chapter 6, the poem "A Une Raison" is seen as central to Rimbaud's "social illuminism" and his celebration of a new epoch of rationality, opposed to superstition and obscurantism. The section ends with a study of the *Illuminations* text, of uncertain date, "Démocratie."

Part IV deals with nine poems, examined through a range of Freudian and post-Freudian concepts, beginning with infantile aggression in "Après le déluge" (chapter 7). This is the poem traditionally placed first in editions of the *Illuminations*. It is followed in chapter 8 by readings of Rimbaud's two darkest poems: "Honte" and "Angoisse." Rhythm is the vehicle of cathartic resolution—or *abreaction*—in these poems. In order to illustrate the universality of abreaction as a feature of literary response, the gloom of "Honte" and "Angoisse" is followed by the enthusiasm of the much-loved poem, "Aube." In all three of these poems, the rhythmical aspect is taken as key to the way they call forth and then "abreact" emotion. Chapter 9 studies the play of fantasy and dream work in "Vies: I, II, III" and the obscure poem "H," generally recognized as an account of masturbation. Chapter 10 presents the greatest of Rimbaud's enigma poems, "Conte," seen side by side with its Baudelairean intertext, "Une Mort héroique." After reviewing some of the multifarious readings of this seemingly transparent poem, I offer my own solution to the enigma. The section ends with a study of "Nocturne vulgaire," a poem of light and dark, that uses the Jack and the Beanstalk story to evoke a child caught between the paternal and maternal imagos. Here, I have resorted to the theory of Melanie Klein, on the ambivalence of infantile desires, to account for the poem's kaleidoscopic vision. What Klein calls "the paranoid position" is a common infantile anxiety. The fact that "Nocturne vulgaire" is traditionally viewed as a hashish dream supports this reading, since mind-altering drugs often produce psychotic states.

Part V presents two poems from *Illuminations*. Chapter 12 studies "Génie," held by many readers to be Rimbaud's finest single work. I propose a new answer to the disputed question of the Génie's identity. Chapter 13 is a discussion of "Solde," a poem that echoes, in a negative register, the high moral tone of "Génie." In it, Rimbaud cries, "A vendre! / For sale!" and offers all that he most values. He mocks the commercialism of the age and the cheapening of art and love. In nineteenth-century France, you can have it all! If there is "narcissistic gain" in the poem (a possible motive for writing it), this is attained by mocking the venality of "the muck and glory of innumerable generations of idiots" whom he had savaged in the "Lettre du voyant." Rimbaud stayed true to his original inspiration and in this late work (André Guyaux places it last among the *Illuminations*) proudly affirms that he never wrote for hire.

Part VI contains two chapters. The first of these (chapter 14) reviews the concept of indeterminacy in the *Illuminations*, as highlighted by Marjorie Perloff in her 1981 book.[8] Perloff finds that Rimbaud "no longer believes in the efficacy of the symbol" (65) and denies that his poem "Villes II" has any stable meaning. My own analysis of the poem uncovers a jubilant "plaisir du texte / textual pleasure" that intersects with a Heideggerean way of seeing "entities"—Rimbaud's ontology.

Finally, my longest chapter reconsiders *Une Saison en enfer* as a working through by sublimation of Rimbaud's conflicted life—his failed cohabitation with Verlaine, the "folly" of *Voyance*, and the burden of his parents and his past, notably his indoctrination as a Catholic child. Out of this comes a hard-won reconciliation.

An appendix, seen from the perspective of my visit to Marseilles and L'Hôpital de la Conception in 1949 (the hospital has been largely rebuilt since that time), recounts the long agony of Rimbaud's illness and death. I see Isabelle Rimbaud, later the fabricator of distortions and downright lies about her brother, as the tutelary spirit or *bodhisattva* who accompanied him during this time; and I try, in a frankly novelistic excursus, to reconstruct Rimbaud's deathbed confession to the hospital chaplain, Canon A. Chaulier.[9]

A Note on the Texts

Page numbers to works cited are given in the text after the first endnoted occurrence.

While writing this book I have kept in mind André Guyaux's seminal work on the *Illuminations*.[10] Guyaux shows that there are vestiges of order in the manuscripts, although Rimbaud's aim of making a fully collated collection was never realized. The poems remain "fragments" and are therefore susceptible to the thematic presentation I use here. All texts are from the reedited version of the *Oeuvres* (2000) by Suzanne Bernard and André Guyaux.

All translations from the poetry of Rimbaud are my own. Excerpts from theoretical and critical works are given in English. Most translations from the French are my own, unless otherwise indicated.

1

"His Day!"*

---

* Headings to each Part are from the poem "Génie."

Overview

Rimbaud and Psychocriticism

> The language of desire is veiled and does not show itself openly. To read its indirections, to account for its effects, is no simple matter. What is at issue?
>
> —Elizabeth Wright[1]

C. A. Hackett's book *Rimbaud l'enfant* (1948) opened a new era in Rimbaud studies.[2] Hackett took as his point of departure this citation from Baudelaire: "Each of a child's minor troubles, each small pleasure, excessively enlarged by an exquisite sensibility, these later become in the adult man, even when he is unaware, the origin of the work of art."[3] Applying this to Rimbaud, Hackett writes: "Incapable of understanding him, his parents transformed him into a monster. They crushed a life that, by the very marvel of its blossoming, terrified them" (162).

Yves Bonnefoy's *Rimbaud* (1961, 1994) went on to illuminate Rimbaud's relationship with his mother and its psychic cost.[4] Bonnefoy writes:

> His mother, who should have been drawn closer to her child by affection and informed by his mere physical presence, became opaque, a being of sinister mystery. And so it is the entire daily world, everything humanized, all that the social group employs for its goals, presumably goals of love—it is places, dwellings, objects that become hostile—and grimace. The grotesque, the sordid, the excremental will appear among these ruins. (14)

Rimbaud was condemned by his own lucidity: "He can try by travel to rediscover the land of marvels; by *the reasoned disorder of all the senses* to awaken in his flesh its natural immediacy, [yet] he will always carry with him the self disgust spoken in 'Honte,' and with it the unsolvable contradictions of his soul and his body" (19; emphasis in original). Bonnefoy's insights into the life and spirit of Rimbaud manifest the empathy of one great poet for another.

The "contradictions" of Rimbaud continue to solicit new approaches to his life and work since the pioneering role of C. A. Hackett and Yves Bonnefoy. Other critics, of a newer generation, have taken Rimbaud's hermeticism and indirection as features that call for an approach through depth psychology. The most adept American psychoanalytic critic is Leo Bersani.

In an influential essay, "The Simplicity of Rimbaud," in his book *A Future for Astyanax,* Bersani writes of "Rimbaud's self-negation."[5] He adds: "Rimbaud seems to have wanted to do away with his own personality as a historical self and to make of this the basis of a universal revolution." Bersani sees the poems, especially the *Illuminations,* as hallucinatory scenes unified only by the disembodied voice of the poet. In a critical discourse, whose mobility almost equals that of the poet, Bersani states: "What Rimbaud's theatricalizing bias eliminates is the sort of continuity—the psychological inferences—provided by a reflective subjectivity" (255). A less cogent view of Rimbaud's psyche as shattered and dispersed—based on the dazzling polyvalence of the *Illuminations*—crops up again when George Steiner writes of "Rimbaud's pulverization of psychic cohesion into charged fragments of centrifugal and transient energy."[6] Finally, the biography of Rimbaud by Graham Robb, published in the year 2000,[7] tends to reinforce this extreme view of the poet as a man lacking equilibrium and out of control, an exhibitionist, a man headed for what Pierre Brunel calls, in his study of Rimbaud, "l'éclatant désastre / the dazzling disaster."[8]

Against these dispersive views of Rimbaud, I place the position of psychoanalyst Daniel Lagache, who singles out certain dominant individuals as possessors of a *constituting* ego, as opposed to the defensive or *constituted* ego, victim of unconscious forces and automatic behaviors. On both the conscious and unconscious levels, Rimbaud was able to dominate the centrifugal forces of his personality. Lagache's position, an outgrowth of later Freudianism, has served to ground my analysis of the dynamic and affirmative aspects of the *Illuminations.*

In a later book, *The Culture of Redemption,*[9] Bersani explores sublimation, repression, and reaction formation in commentaries on Melanie Klein, Marcel Proust, and, above all, Freud. These are themes that must come into play in any psychoanalytic consideration of Rimbaud; hence, even when he is discussing another writer, such as Genet or Bataille, Bersani remains a major contributor to the critical tradition started by Hackett. Beyond this, the fact that he treats psychoanalytic discourse ("the language of desire") as a subset of literary expression serves to buttress the position taken here, namely, that the language of psychocriticism is always to some degree a type of figurative language. Or, to put it another way, there is a powerful reciprocity between aesthetic form and psychocritical analysis, between psyche and text.[10]

IN HIS *L'Horizon fabuleux* (1988), Michel Collot, following Hussserl's initiative, explores the notion of horizon as constitutive of the entire field of memories, perceptions, experiences out of which any cognitive act arises.[11] Besides the cognitive grounding given by Husserl, Collot also points to the ontological grounding demonstrated by Heidegger. For Arthur Rimbaud anticipated in his life and work a number of the fundamental assumptions that animate the ontology of the German philosopher.

As I continued in this project, probing the poems of Rimbaud and the personality behind those poems, I began to see, in a tentative way, that the radical character of "meaning" in Rimbaud's work *might* be resolved if Rimbaud were to be viewed in a Heideggerean perspective. In "la lettre du voyant / letter of the seer" (*Oeuvres*, 364) Rimbaud begins by praising those same Greek poets in whom Heidegger found the original and authentic description of being ("*physis*"). Rimbaud continues in "la lettre du voyant": "En Grèce, ai-je dit, vers et lyres *rhythment l'Action*." ("In Greece, as I've said, poems and lyres *give rhythm to Action*.") Like Heidegger, he sees the poet as involved with the world (the word "Action" is crucial), not simply submitting to it. Rimbaud's poetic vision embraces the same world-constituting concern (*Sorge* or Care) in which Heidegger was to find the generation of meaning.

Heidegger saw temporality as the horizon of each individual life and, within that horizon, the confrontation with death as the ultimate challenge. As a young poet, Rimbaud was shot and wounded by his partner, Paul Verlaine. *Une Saison en enfer,* produced immediately after that traumatic experience, is Rimbaud's chief "existentialist" work; but many other poems, especially those that deal with risk and death, fall within that horizon. Rimbaud's life, Collot finds, quoting from the poet's "Soleil et chair / Sun and flesh" is repeated displacement: "Et l'horizon s'enfuit d'une fuite éternelle!" ("And the horizon flees in an eternal flight!"). Paul Verlaine called Rimbaud "l'homme aux semelles de vent / the man with shoes of wind," for he was always on the move, in pursuit of a constantly receding horizon. He was looking for what Heidegger, speaking metaphorically, called the *dwelling* or the *house of language,* which might be poetry or one of those "splendides villes / splendid cities" through which Rimbaud passed, till death caught him in mid-stride.[12]

Other critics have also explored the Rimbaldian unconscious. The Italian critic Sergio Sacchi is an example of an aesthetic critic whose point of departure is the juvenile elements that survive in the precocious adolescent. As André Guyaux suggests in the preface to Sacchi's posthumous *Etudes sur 'les Illuminations' de Rimbaud,* Sacchi looks for the transplant of early memories in later poems.[13] He studies the images of dispossessed children, the orphans and vagrants of the early poems, finding in them an oscillation between volition and regret. Sacchi projects into a virtual future Rimbaud's dream of release from temporality. He looks at the narrative gaps and the temporal short circuits that collapse past and present.

Among contemporary French critics of Rimbaud, Jean-Luc Steinmetz is the most Freudian. In an essay on "Mémoire" he writes: "Here then surges up a being (maternal idol, phallic woman, to name her by her ferocious affective titles): *the mother* that Rimbaud can never surrender. It is almost stupefying to see that Rimbaud never truly abandons his mother and that he had *something to tell this woman that he could never get out*" (emphasis in original).[14]

In the *Illumination* "Barbare" Steinmetz identifies the mysterious refrain "Le pavillon en viande saignante sur la soie des mers et des fleurs arctiques (elles n'existent pas) / The flag of bloody meat on the silken seas and arctic flowers (they don't exist)" with the trauma of birth and the forbidden fantasy of incest.[15] His analyses begin with a Freudian theme but always go beyond it.

SINCE HACKETT'S landmark book in 1948, the field of psychocriticism has expanded with the multiplication of post-Freudian theories. Melanie Klein found her point of departure in Freud's instinct theory, yet elaborated her work in a way that was more totally responsive to the complexity of human personality. D. W. Winnicott, with his concept of the transitional object in the mother–child dyad, brought an original approach to the role of the instinctual life in cultural production. There is also Hans Loewald, who expands in more positive fashion the notion of sublimation, treated summarily by Freud. Loewald's book on sublimation has helped me develop a new reading of *Une Saison en enfer*.[16]

THE GREATEST FLAW of psychocriticism is its reductive use of explanatory labels such as "Oedipus complex" or "death wish" or "narcissism," etc.[17] The whole of psychoanalysis can be figured by the trope of "metalepsis," defined as "present effect attributed to a remote cause."[18] Sublimation, as I will suggest in my analysis of *Une Saison en enfer*, is based on chiasmus, the rhetorical figure of crossing. Other psychic tropes will appear as the book unfolds. No matter how reader and writer be construed, the constant of all psychocriticism is the effort to unseal the poetic unconscious by releasing its tropic energy. This happens when a figure from the text reconfigures the term that has been advanced to explain it. By this "transfer," the concept may become a metaphor, that is, a third term combining the other two. So in Rimbaud's "Mémoire," the Valley of the Meuse becomes the conjugal bedroom, with the concept "primal scene" relating the triad back to the poet. This way of reading, with its frequent shifts in register, fuses a psychological reading with the aesthetic.[19] In short, psychocriticism seeks to unlock the energy (i.e., "desire") embedded in figurative language. And it does this in a language that is itself akin to poetry: heavy with myth, redolent with deeds of shame and glory, baptized in violence, dripping with blood; a language that practices the darkest pathways of the soul yet may release the soul from oppression when all hope seems lost.

There is, of course, no way to prove the interpretations of psychocriticism. We can't ask the poet to provide further free associations, we can't interpret the transference and countertransference between the poet and his readers. Psychocriticism, at best, can only *suggest,* basing its inferences on context and repetition of themes and images from poem to poem.

MANY HAVE asked why Rimbaud abandoned poetry and chose instead a life of hardship, the last eleven years spent in Africa trying to make his fortune. He hated Africa; the word "ennui" recurs continually in his letters home. The oppressive heat, the long and dangerous caravans, the tough-minded scoundrels he dealt with, everything conspired against him. Did he abandon poetry because it exacted too great a repressive toll? Or because his concept of poetry involved an unacceptable self-revelation? In the "Adieu" from *Une Saison en enfer* Rimbaud asks: "Mais pourquoi regretter un éternel soleil, si nous sommes engagés à la découverte de la clarté divine,—loin des gens qui meurent sur les saisons?" ("But why regret an eternal sun, if we are committed to the discovery of the divine light,—far from those who die with the seasons?") Here he implies that poetry transcends death. Rimbaud's poetry survived the random scattering of its manuscripts, his own loss of interest ("je ne pense plus à ça / I don't think about that anymore"), and the repudiation of many of his contemporaries who found him "un homme infréquentable / an intolerable man" (Hackett, 42). A century and a half later, his enigmatic texts still hold the promise of clarity to those who search for "le lieu et la formule / the place and the secret."

"He is affection and the present"

2

Defiance in "Les Poètes de sept ans"

This great poem begins with any day in the life of a child:

> Et la Mère, fermant le livre du devoir,
> S'en allait satisfaite et très-fière, sans voir,
> Dans les yeux bleus et sous le front plein d'éminences,
> L'âme de son enfant livrée aux répugnances.

> And the Mother, closing the duty-book,
> Went off satisfied and very proud, not seeing
> In his blue eyes and beneath the bumpy forehead
> Her child's soul given up to loathing.

The initial conjunction "Et" implies the ongoing nature of a conflict between mother and child, one of which she is not even aware. After all, she has told him his duties, thereby fulfilling her role; and she goes away satisfied, not seeing the defiance in his eyes, the wretchedness in his soul. If he is to reach maturity with an adequate sense of wholeness and self-respect, the loathing must not overcome the defiance. Only if he finds strength to confront this woman whom he called sarcastically "la Bouche d'ombre / the Mouth of shadow" will he be a survivor.[1]

D. M. Winnicott writes of " . . . the correspondence between a mother's behavior and the 'cathected internal mother imago. . . . ' " [*This means the identity or the difference between the mother's real world behavior and the mother as construed in the child's psyche and in whom he has invested his psychic energy*]. Winnicott argues that when the mother (the child's first object) betrays in some way his love and trust, as does Mme Rimbaud, then the child loses his grasp of the reality principle, his relation with the world. On the other hand: "The capacity for object-relationships having become established, the child can now proceed to such things as obedience, defiance and identification" (472).

Defiance and anger were Rimbaud's refuge, his strength in the daily battle with his mother; and "Les Poètes de sept ans," written when he was seventeen, recounts an early phase of that conflict, when he first began to fight for his very existence and his place in the world as an autonomous being:

> Tout le jour il suait d'obéissance; très
> Intelligent: pourtant des tics noirs, quelques traits
> Semblaient prouver en lui d'âcres hypocrisies.
> Dans l'ombre des couloirs aux teintures moisies,
> En passant il tirait la langue, les deux poings
> A l'aine, et dans ses yeux fermés voyait des points.

> All day long he sweated obedience; very
> Intelligent: but black obsessions, mannerisms,
> Seemed to prove bitter hypocrisies.
> Passing through shadowed halls with moldy
> Walls, he stuck out his tongue, stuck two fists
> In his groin, and squinted till he saw spots.

This is compulsion; obedience makes him sweat, his only reward what he has already heard a thousand times: "What an intelligent child!" But it's all hypocrisy, and after a line about the mildewed wallpaper that gives an unpleasant picture of Mme Rimbaud's house, we learn how the child takes his revenge: he sticks out his tongue and squints till he sees spots in front of his eyes—already at age seven he is practicing *Voyance!* It is during this time, around puberty, that, in Bonnefoy's memorable phrase: "The child experiences the emptiness of signs, their mendacity" (14). This emptiness of signs is a determining factor in the development of Rimbaud's poetry; it accounts for the aesthetic of "indeterminism" that is found in the *Illuminations*. Reacting against "the great emotional lie" of his bigoted mother, Rimbaud finds truth in nature, where the excremental and the ugly provide a refuge from "the ignoble game of the ideal" (Bonnefoy, 17). But there is a true light in nature that "dissolves the signs of opacity." These two extremes combine in this passage from the draft of *Une Saison en enfer*: "Je restais de longues heures la langue pendante, comme les bêtes harassées: je me traînais dans les ruelles puantes, et, les yeux fermés, je m'offrais au soleil, Dieu de feu. . . . / I remained many hours my tongue hanging out, like a tormented animal; I dragged myself through stinking streets and, eyes closed, I offered myself to the sun, god of fire . . . " (Pléiade, 168).

It is here that Bonnefoy finds a Gnostic current in Rimbaud. He connects Rimbaud with Nietzsche, although Rimbaud never read the philosopher, ten years his senior; nor is it apparent that he knew anything about Zarathustra, devotee of Mazda, worshiper of fire, whom Nietzsche chose as his spiritual ancestor.[2] I suggest that the closest parallel with Nietzsche is that in *Voyance* Rimbaud is exercising a will to power, an "overcoming of oneself," as Nietzsche announced his own program in *Thus Spoke Zarathustra*.

RIMBAUD'S SEARCH for meaning in the reinvention of language is very different from Nietzsche's search for values, although like Nietzsche he came to despise Christianity. In the eyes of Heidegger, Nietzsche is a Platonist; he sees values as preexisting. In the words of Herbert L. Dreyfus:

> Once we get the idea that there is a plurality of values and that we choose which ones will have a claim on us, we are ripe for the modern idea, first found in the works of Nietzsche, especially in *Thus Spoke Zarathustra*, that we *posit* our values—that is, that valuing is something we do and value is the result of doing it. . . . As Heidegger says, "No one dies for mere values." (emphasis in original)[3]

Rimbaud's commitment to poetry, as a transcendent power that must go beyond the seeming emptiness of signs to the hidden reality of things, is akin to Heidegger's "disclosure" of the being of entities as it arises in experience. Bonnefoy finds the parallel with Nietzsche in "Soleil et chair," with its celebration of sensuality; yet that poem is heavy with borrowed allegory and lacks the authentic warmth and spontaneity of poems such as "Au Cabaret vert" and "Ma Bohême." What Rimbaud discovers in his passionate search for knowledge is not the Gnosticism of Nietzsche (the cult of Mazda) so much as a relearning of the relation between words and objects, a relation falsified for him by the duplicity of his mother.

In this environment dominated by "la mother" (one of his insulting pseudonyms for Mme Rimbaud), Sunday is colorless and oppressive. The children are compelled to read from the Bible, no doubt the seventeenth-century version of Maistre de Sacy, translated from the Vulgate.[4] This provincial Catholicism, with its soot-coated statues and *ex votos,* its reliquaries and bleeding hearts, amounts to an enforced Gnosis, if we consider Gnosis to be a secret or special knowledge, limited to members of a sect. How could this child, hungry for affection, love the God who is his mother's bogey-man, her second-in-command? Instead he loves his own absent father, incarnate in all the workingmen who return home in the evening, always ready with a greeting or a smile. Here Rimbaud is discovering the solidarity to which he is immediately and intuitively committed: the workingmen, the public square where, amid the crowd's derision, the Emperor's edicts are read aloud. These crowds suggest the swell of Fenimore Cooper's prairies and these in turn the tumescence of puberty. "Les Poètes de sept ans" ends with a retreat to darkness, humidity and again a premonition of *Voyance:*

> Et comme il savourait surtout les sombres choses,
> Quand, dans la chambre nue aux persiennes closes,
> Haute et bleue, âcrement prise d'humidité,
> Il lisait son roman sans cesse médité,
> Plein de lourds ciels ocreux et de forêts noyées,
> De fleurs de chair aux bois sidérals déployées,
> Vertige, écroulements, déroutes et pitié!
> —Tandis que se faisait la rumeur du quartier,
> En bas,—seul, et couché sur des pièces de toile
> Ecrue, et pressentant violemment la voile!

> And since he especially savored somber things,
> When, in the bare room with drawn shutters,
> High and blue, with its penetrating damp,
> He read his novel endlessly recalled,
> Full of heavy ochre skies and drowning forests,
> Flowers of flesh dispersed in astral woods,
> Vertigo, collapse, and piteous defeats!
> —While the hum of the neighborhood goes on
> Outside,—he's all alone, stretched on bleached
> Canvas scraps, violently announcing sails!

This is *Voyance*—a concrete act, to simulate his escape to freedom; he lies on scraps of canvas and (an imaginary) wind lifts his sails! There is another anticipation of *Voyance* earlier in the poem:

>   L'été
> Surtout, vaincu, stupide, il était entêté
> A se renfermer dans la fraîcheur des latrines:
> Il pensait là, tranquille et livrant ses narines.

>   In summer
> Defeated, stupid, he liked best
> To lock himself within the coolness of latrines;
> He could think there, in peace and breathe deep.

This is the attraction of "l'immondice / filth," referred to earlier, the factuality of nature as opposed to the false idealism and pretension of his mother. Here Rimbaud anticipates Proust, and how many other pubescent children?

YVES BONNEFOY has shown us that "Les Poetes de sept ans" is a document of central importance for understanding Rimbaud. It shows us *Voyance* in its initial phases and, implicit in those larval beginnings, the origins of a philosophical project that will reach maturity with Martin Heidegger.

It should not strike the reader as anomalous that a nineteenth-century French adolescent pursued the path taken by a mature philosopher some sixty-five years later. Both pursued truth in the dance of existence, the "mirror-play of world"; both fought against the fettering of convention; both were visionaries who, to use the philosopher's words, looked into the "unconcealedness" of beings, "the lighting-clearing of the There," and introduced it "as a place of the sort in which each being emerges or arises in its own way."[5]

3

Poem of the Uncanny

"Le Bateau ivre"

"Le Bateau ivre" opens like a classic horror film. The adverbial phrase "comme je descendais / as I fled down..." plunges the reader into an action manifestly *against nature*—down "fleuves impassibles / impassible rivers"; but it is the passive position sustained throughout the poem that most clearly identifies it with horror. The boat is no longer "guidé par les haleurs / guided by the haulers" but loosed into the waves. To be held and cradled is reassuring for an infant, but for a small craft in redskin country, passivity is an invitation to danger. The poet makes the infantile reference and introduces a note of anxiety:

> Dans les clapotements furieux des marées,
> Moi, l'autre hiver, plus sourd que les cerveaux d'enfants,
> Je courus! Et les Péninsules démarrées
> N'ont pas subi tohu-bohus plus triomphants.
>
> In the furious surging of the tides,
> More heedless than babies' brains, last winter
> I ran! and no Peninsulas set loose
> Have known such carnivals of triumph.

This "tohu-bohu" is more violent than any invented by earlier Romantic or Parnassian poets, for "Bateau ivre" is meant to be a new kind of poem, written for Verlaine and the Parisian poets Rimbaud was soon to meet. It is also an indicator of a psychic process—the uncanny—at work in the poem.[1] Indeed, the basic format of the poem—*the speaking boat*—corresponds to the first feature that Freud ascribes to the uncanny, the uncertainty as to "whether a particular figure is a real person or an automaton [or an inanimate object]." Freud adds that the reader's "attention is not focused directly on the uncertainty, lest he should be prompted to examine and settle the matter at once, for in this way, as we have said, the special emotional effect can be easily dissipated."[2]

"VOILÀ CE QUE j'ai fait pour leur présenter, / Here is what I wrote to show them," Rimbaud told his friend Delahaye. And he added, after reading the poem aloud, "Ah oui, on n'a rien écrit encore de semblable, je le sais bien / Yes indeed, nobody has ever written anything to equal this, I know for a fact."

The poem is astonishing in many respects; for one thing, it is the first major work of Rimbaud's to put into effect his notion of *Voyance*. When he wrote "Le Bateau ivre," he was living out his self-imposed system of personal and moral hygiene, and the poem is in effect a report on the results obtained by that devastating regimen. In the preceding two years, Rimbaud had undergone a process of intellectual and spiritual conditioning, under the influence of great post-Enlightenment thinkers, such as Victor Hugo, Jules Michelet, and Edgar Quinet. At the time he wrote his "Lettres du voyant" to his friend, Paul Demeny, and his teacher, Georges Izambard, Rimbaud had added a moral dimension to his program.

During the winter of 1870–71 his whole appearance changed. His hair had been long, but now it reached his shoulders; he slouched and scowled, his face broke out with acne. This was the time he chalked "Mort à Dieu!" on the town benches and muttered insults whenever he met a priest. He walked like a robot, talked to himself, used drugs when he could get them, and bragged to Izambard of his debauchery: "Je me fais cyniquement entretenir; je déterre d'anciens imbéciles de collège; tout ce que je pouvais inventer de bête, de sale, de mauvais, en action et en paroles, je le leur livre, on me paie en bocks et en filles / Cynically, I'm being kept; I dig up old imbeciles from school; I feed them with anything I can invent that's stupid, filthy, bad, in act and words, I dish it out to them and they pay me in beer and in whores" (Pléiade xxi). He surrendered to the addictive power of "l'absomphe" (absinthe), the way the drunken boat surrenders to the waves. All this with the aim of unleashing the power to *see*:

Je m'habituai à l'hallucination simple: je voyais très franchement une mosquée à la place d'une usine, une école de tambours faite par des anges, des calèches sur les routes du ciel, un salon au fond d'un lac . . .

I practiced simple hallucination: I frankly saw a mosque in place of a factory, a drum school made by angels, buggies on the roads of heaven, a parlor at the bottom of a lake. . . . (*Oeuvres,* 225)

Given the limited resources of Roche and the surrounding countryside, it couldn't have been easy to "s'encrapuler et de rechercher toutes les formes d'amour, de souffrance, de folie . . . / to crap out and seek all forms of love, of suffering, of madness . . . " (*Oeuvres,* 455). A village in the Ardennes is not the preferred place to engage in world-class dissipation. Still, he pursued *Voyance* so resolutely that his young sisters were terrified and his mother decided he'd gone crazy. His guide to debauchery was Charles Bretagne, an older man who was, in the words of Enid Starkie, "notorious and infamous for his blasphemous opinions and for being the fiercest and most voracious *mangeur de curés* (priest-hater)"[3] (98). It appears likely that there was also what Lefrère calls "un trait de complicité homosexuelle / an element of homosexual complicity" in Bretagne's involvement with Rimbaud,[4] ending with the eventual recommendation of the teenage poet to Verlaine.

When the famous meeting took place, the second or third week of September 1871, Rimbaud had cut his hair and cleaned himself up, but he still appeared as an awkward rustic, with a heavy Ardennais accent. He managed for a time to control the aggressivity and insolence that defined his behavior in Charleville, but once he settled down in Paris these characteristics reasserted themselves.

The issue is not whether this "dérèglement raisonné de tous les sens / reasoned disordering of all the senses" helped refine Rimbaud's poetic talent or, more likely, had the opposite effect. Rimbaud's genius was an unquenchable daemon, the kind of natural endowment that occurs only once or twice a century. *Voyance* was a form of theatricality, designed to provide a persona to house the genius within. This behavior, that he himself called "effroyablement abject / frightfully abject," was part of the cost of genius.

IN PARALLEL with his own personal doctrine of *Voyance,* Rimbaud combines the theme of the uncanny, already implicit in the work of Victor

Hugo and Baudelaire. The uncanny manifests as the foreign, the dangerous, the haunting; and, indeed, in "Le Bateau ivre" the reader is haunted by echoes from Poe, from Jules Verne, from the Bible, and from Hugo himself. In its simplest sense, the uncanny is an emotion that accompanies the surfacing of a childhood terror. Here it is the fear of being dropped or thrown, poetically represented by the drunken boat tossed on the waves.

JAMES LAWLER'S study of "Le Bateau ivre" emphasizes the many ways in which it echoes and competes with Baudelaire's "Le Voyage."[5] Baudelaire's masterpiece provides a controlling frame of reference for "Le Bateau ivre"; it is a work to emulate and even surpass. Both are written in alternately rhyming alexandrine quatrains. Both explore the theme of voyage, although to contrasting ends. Baudelaire surveys the voyage of life with a world-weary gaze. Rimbaud invents a nightmare landscape that bruises its hapless victim with forces beyond his control. The poem explodes with images from multiple sources, for, even during this period of dissipation, Rimbaud retained the ability to recall and recast a vast array of readings. Images emerge and fuse into one soaring crescendo after another as the boat, loosened from human agency, rises toward "les cieux crevant en éclairs" ("skies shattering with lightning") only to plunge into "Echouages hideux au fond des golfes bruns / Où les serpents géants dévorés des punaises / Choient, des arbres tordus, avec de noirs parfums!" / "Hideous strands at the bottom of brown gulfs / Where giant snakes ravaged by bedbugs / Tumble from gnarled trees with black perfumes!"

Rimbaud's imagery is not merely exotic or picturesque. The uncanny works at both the narrative and the figurative levels. The boat sees " . . . le soleil bas, taché d'horreurs mystiques / Illuminant de long figements violets / Pareils à des acteurs de drames très-antiques / Les flots roulant au loin leurs frissons de volets!" / " . . . the setting sun, stained with mystic horrors / Lighting with long violet clots / Similar to actors in very ancient dramas / The waves afar rolling their shutter-like clatter!"

In his essay on Hoffman's *Sandman*, where Freud analyzes the uncanny, "seeing" is at issue; and in "Le Bateau ivre" the poet-boat is both seer and seen by "l'oeil niais des falots / the silly eye of lanterns" and the "yeux de panthères à peaux / d'homme" / "eyes of panthers with human skins."

All the eyes that he passes by, of buoys and panthers and birds, threaten him as do the incredible sounds of "Le rut des Béhémots et les Maelstroms épais . . . / "The rutting of Behemoths and the density of Maelstroms. . . . " The eyes of the poet-boat are threatened by these other-worldly sights and sounds; though it is, along with the threat of castration, as in Freud, the equal threat of being thrown out of the cradle, of being catapulted into the "brumes violettes / violet fogs" or the "ciel rougeoyant comme un mur / the sky reddening like a wall." Here Rimbaud has captured in image and rhythm the primal images that haunt a human child, images that surpass the fears they name—castration, rejection, ejection—and encompass the fundamental terror of the species.

The poem can be seen as one wildly varied repetition compulsion—the tendency of an instinct to manifest (albeit in disguise) over and over again. The passive boat, surrendered to the forces of nature, represents the pre-oedipal child at that moment when he is most vulnerable to terror. The boat is tossed and threatened by sea monsters and wild animals, driven to far horizons where it glides past glaciers, while sounds crash around it, as if intoned by some unearthly chorale. Here, in this powerful music, is the "omnipotence of thought," defined by Freud as yet another element of the uncanny.

The poem's sea monsters and wild animals, its far horizons, its Saintes Maries de la Mer, its glaciers and its drowned cadavers, all contribute to the verbal–visual chorale that engulfs the boat and threatens to overwhelm it as frail craft and sea together follow their frenzied course. The sensation is not so much that the boat will be swamped or crushed by the waves; for the chaos is obedient to the disembodied voice—like a conductor's baton—that leads its orchestra of mad players. The voice is the boat but also the frenzied conductor who seems to rise out of the watery element that he leads through its roiling exertions. For this is the "Poem of the Sea"—but also the "Sea of the Poem"—where language becomes (to use Conrad's phrase) the *destructive element*. It is here, as nowhere else in all of Rimbaud's poetry, that we find his verbal magic unleashed to its full diapason. It was Verlaine's favorite among all his friend's poems. He wrote of it: " . . . ce maître morceau vous prend par sa toute-beauté de forme et vous courbe sous sa toute-puissance d'originalité. Est-ce bien l'âme de l'homme ou la libre fantaisie du poète qui est en jeu, qu'importe! C'est d'une suprême grandeur dans la plus neuve des mises en oeuvres . . . " / " . . . this masterful piece seizes you by its entire-beauty of form and bends you to its entire-beauty of originality. Is the soul of the man or the poet's unbounded fantasy at stake! no matter! The work is one of supreme grandeur in the newest of presentations. . . . "[6]

Chapter 3. Poem of the Uncanny: "Le Bateau ivre"

RIMBAUD'S IMAGINATION has its tender moments, as in "Mémoire," its lyrical moments, as in "L'Eternité." It is capable of many effects, but in "Le Bateau ivre" it reaches a crescendo like that of Berlioz's *Symphonie Fantastique*. In such a work the closural question arises: how bring it to an end? Can "Le Voyage" serve as a guide? Baudelaire's poem lacks the metaphorical exuberance of "Le Bateau ivre." An important difference between the two is that Rimbaud, following the program of *Voyance,* seeks to communicate auditory and visual sensations through the play of language, while Baudelaire's visual scenes are interspersed with ironic intellectualization, until the final diptych recapitulates: "Plonger au fond du gouffre, Enfer ou Ciel, qu'importe? / Au fond de l'Inconnu pour trouver du *nouveau!*" / "Plunge to the bottom of the abyss, Hell or Heaven, what does it matter? / To the bottom of the Unknown to find *novelty!*"; emphasis in original) In this conclusion, the jaded hedonist asks no more than novelty. Baudelaire's traveler might be sitting in a well-appointed bar room, gazing into his cocktail glass. When asked: "Dites, qu'avez-vous vu? / Tell me, what have you seen?" he replies:

> Nous avons vu des astres
> Et des flots; nous avons vu des sables aussi;
> Et malgré bien des chocs et d'imprévus désastres,
> Nous nous sommes souvent ennuyés, comme ici.

> We have seen stars
> And waves; we have seen sands as well;
> And in spite of many shocks and unforeseen disasters,
> We have often been just as bored as we are here.

"Le Voyage" lacks the accelerating rhythm, the breathless suspense as we leap from one image to the next, the hallucinatory frenzy of "Le Bateau ivre." The principal difference between the two poems is that Rimbaud reaches the domain of the uncanny—dismemberment, death—while Baudelaire prefers the lower key of irony.

HOW ACHIEVE closure, how descend from such a pitch of emotion? This brings us to the central problematic of "Le Bateau ivre"—the unexpected "dissolve" that occurs in the last five stanzas. Tossed high on the waves, spectator of hallucinatory sights and sounds, the talking boat—"Fileur éternel des immobilités bleues / Eternal spinner of blue immobilities"— announces abruptly: "Je regrette l'Europe aux anciens parapets!" ("I miss Europe with its ancient parapets!")

Why this nostalgia, this sudden return to reality? It is not simply a convenient way to end the poem, an interruption to the paratactic litany of tumultuous images; it is too sudden, too unexpected. It breaks through from a region totally outside the poem, with the force of revelation of the inner life of the poet. Here the poet himself becomes aware of the presence of the uncanny. Neil Hertz writes: "The feeling of the uncanny would seem to be generated by being-reminded-of-the-repetition-compulsion, not by being-reminded-of-whatever-it-is-that-is-repeated. It is the becoming aware of the process that is felt as eerie, not the becoming aware of some particular item in the unconscious, once familiar, then repressed, now coming back into consciousness."[7]

The uncanny intrudes on the margin of consciousness as the poem builds to its climax. The repressed memory of being shaken, dropped, or thrown away—or perhaps all of these at once—returns in the first verse of the twenty-first stanza:

> Moi qui tremblais, sentant geindre à cinquante lieues
> Le rut des Béhémots et les Maelstroms épais,
> Fileur éternel des immobilités bleues,
> Je regrette l'Europe aux anciens parapets!
>
> I who trembled hearing at fifty leagues off
> The rutting of Behemoths and the dense Maelstroms,
> Eternal spinner of blue immobilities,
> I miss Europe with its ancient parapets!

At this point the *passive* suffering of the poet-boat breaks the boundary of consciousness and it is stricken with a nameless sorrow: "Je regrette l'Europe aux anciens parapets!"

This world traveler, this "homme aux semelles de vent / man with shoes of wind," as Verlaine called him, always returned home to the family farm at Roche, to his mother and his siblings. Whenever he was sick, broke, discouraged, this banal countryside, so often disparaged and insulted ("Charlestown, un sale trou / a filthy hole," etc.), drew him back. In "Le Bateau ivre," within the imagined space of the boat's drunken journey, he hears the summons again. In the *fictive* time of the poem, the

Chapter 3. Poem of the Uncanny: "Le Bateau ivre"

speaker dreams of home; in the *psychic* time of the poem's composition, he turns back from the excess of *Voyance*.

> Est-ce en ces nuits sans fond que tu dors et t'exiles,
> Million d'oiseaux d'or, ô future Vigueur?—
>
> Is it in these endless nights that you sleep exiled,
> A million golden birds, O future Vigor?

The poet has just displayed great vigor in his ability to generate the powerful images of the poem; but this is not enough even though he had dreamed of it, punished himself to achieve it. Vigor with a capital "V" means the future energy of mankind put to productive use in a new democratic society, as envisaged by the ideologues of the century. But even that is not enough; and the next stanza moves us into an entirely different context:

> Mais, vrai, j'ai trop pleuré! Les Aubes sont navrantes.
> Toute lune est atroce et tout soleil amer:
> L'acre amour m'a gonflé de torpeurs enivrantes.
> O que ma quille éclate! O que j'aille à la mer!
>
> I've wept too much, it's true! The Dawns break my heart.
> Every moon is atrocious and each sun is bitter.
> Acrid love has pumped me with drugged torpor.
> O let my keel burst, let me go to the sea!

Several critics have remarked that it is no longer the boat speaking, but Rimbaud himself. It is as if he steps out of the frame of the poem and into a black and white photograph of a small boy, who launches a paper boat into a puddle. He is inexplicably sad: "Un enfant accroupi plein de tristesses . . . / A crouching child full of sadness. . . . " He longs for the love (like a million golden birds) that he may once have known fleetingly but will never know again. That memory fades as threatening eyes watch him: "Je ne puis plus . . . nager sous les yeux horribles des pontons / I can no longer . . . swim under the horrible eyes of prison scows."[8]

He has faced the uncanny yet cannot sustain a prolonged confrontation. But at least he has encountered the reality principle and rediscovered his own world. Reassured by this familiarity, there is also sadness at the magic that he must relinquish. We will encounter other poems where the restoration of the real is accompanied by sadness; this is a sign of loss, and of the tragedy of Rimbaud's life as a man. We also meet in "Le Bateau ivre" a powerful new way of describing objects, a way that reveals both their illusory character (i.e., they cannot satisfy desire), and the way in which they reveal the human self as what, some sixty-five years after Rimbaud, Heidegger called "the being toward death."[9]

4

Figures of Desire in "Mémoire"

"Mémoire" is an Ovidian poem of metamorphosis. As the Meuse river follows its course, sketched by the pen of memory, figures emerge in varied shapes, evolve and change, sinking again into oblivion as ". . . l'eau limpide et captive de sa profondeur tourne lentement sur elle-même / . . . the limpid and captive water laps slowly upon itself."[1] Atle Kittang has seen the poem as a flight from meaning: "the withdrawal of the signified and the leveling of the order of meaning"[2]; or, contrastively, it is read as an exploration of memory by James Lawler.[3] My approach here is motivated by the fact that Rimbaud himself linked the poem with *Voyance* in its most deadly phase: "Les hallucinations étant plus vives, la terreur venait! Je faisais des sommeils de plusieurs jours, et, levé, continuais les rêves les plus tristes, égaré partout / As the hallucinations became more intense, terror overcame me! I slept for several days in a row, and awakened, continued the saddest dreams, desperate wherever I turned."[4] For here memory is not an autonomous process but is linked with the deepest aspects of emotional life; it is inscribed as both character and destiny. In this respect, Ross Chambers's comparison with "Ophélie," written two years earlier in 1870, is instructive.[5] Chambers sees both texts as based on "l'écoulement / flowing." Yet the literary subject and the Parnassian borrowings of the earlier poem place a filter (Chambers speaks of a "dream"; 25) between the text and the immediacy of sensation. Of the multiple readings of

"Mémoire," Chambers comes closest to capturing the "expressive system of the text" (23) in the limpidity of his interpretation.

The flowing river murmurs in the poem's phonetic structure. In stanza 1 and again in stanza 2, we hear repeated vowel sounds: *eau, assaut, soie, bras; carreau, bouillons, eau, oiseaux,* etc. These suggest that form of song called *"vocalise,"* defined as a voice exercise upon one or two related vowels.[6] Taken with the feminine end rhymes and the interjections (Eh! and ô in Part II, Hélas in III, oh! and Ah! in Part V), the poem has the immediacy of music. It is a "pensée chantée et *comprise* du chanteur / a thought sung and understood by the singer" (Letter to Demeny, 15 May, 1871).

"Mémoire" is as much a word painting as it is a song. It opens with a landscape outlined in broad strokes; upon this ground, figures arise. They emerge from the river and surrounding hills. There are women wading or washing, whose partial nudity assaults the eyes with desire. In the second stanza of Part I the broken rhythm announces a metamorphosis: "l'ébat des anges; Non . . . le courant d'or en marche, meut ses bras, noirs, et lourds, et frais surtout, d'herbe . . . / the play of angels; No . . . the golden current flowing, moves its arms, black and heavy, above all cool, with grass. . . . " The River swells and becomes immense, taking the entire valley for her bedroom (Elle / sombre, ayant le Ciel bleu pour ciel-de-lit, appelle / pour rideaux l'ombre de la colline et de l'arche . . . " / "She, somber, taking the blue Sky for her canopy, calls up / for curtains the shadow of the hill and of the arch"); but then, in Part III, she shrinks to become a familiar figure: "Madame se tient trop debout dans la prairie / Madame stands too straight in the field."

It should not surprise us to find the feminine imago playing a dominant role in Rimbaud's imagination. Using a *pointilliste* technique, "Mémoire" seems to convey the free play of perception; yet this *apparent* freedom actually shows how memory shapes the inner world according to an archtypical matrix, neither hallucination nor dream but a decisive reality.

We can never be neutral observers of life. So the poet, who first speaks as casual dreamer, finds his vision shaped by past experience that he only dimly remembers. In an essay on the *Illuminations,* Leo Bersani discusses "this floating, unanchored quality of objects (or attributes or concepts) in Rimbaud's visions. . . . " Bersani comments: "It seems to me that the floating-asociability of Rimbaud's fragmented world excludes *all* systems of definition. . . . The *Illuminations* point toward a revolutionized consciousness precisely to the extent that Rimbaud substitutes fragmented vision for any conceptualizing definitions at all."[7] Yet Rimbaud's freedom and the seeming randomness of memory is only an illusion, even though, by comparison with the earlier poem—"Ophélie"—this work surely inclines further toward fragmentation. The poem begins with images that seem free-floating, autonomous; yet, driven by the habitual patterns of memory, it begins, in Parts II and III, to coalesce into a version of the Freudian family romance.[8]

"MÉMOIRE" OPENS with the emergence of a landscape or background. Water resolves into bright arrows of sunshine from silken bodies. In line three, lilies and banners glorify the Maid. Why *"la pucelle"*? Kleinian psychoanalysis shows how the ego splits its images in order to manage them, dividing them into good and bad, loved and feared, libidinal and aggressive.[9] The Jeanne d'Arc we first encounter in the poem is merely the first of the many roles played by the feminine persona who dominates "Mémoire." The poet sees her as St. Joan, defending the ramparts. Then she is the water again, gold, moving torpid limbs. This multiple Being (River and Woman) takes the valley for her bedroom, as she calls upon the arching hills to veil her couch. At this point the immense female figure dominates sky and valley, engulfing the drama of her son.

PART II begins with an exhaled breath "Eh!" joining air and running water in a sensation both seen and heard. Rising bubbles gild the beds of girls, perhaps Vitalie and Isabelle, Rimbaud's sisters, whose skirts are vivid among the willows, where the sunshine diffuses like a flight of birds. The second stanza of Part II begins with pure sensation, then opens into the heart of a drama, monumental in scope to the mind of a child:

> Plus pure qu'un louis, jaune et chaude paupière
> le souci d'eau—ta foi conjugale, ô l'Epouse!—
> au midi prompt, de son terne miroir, jalouse
> au ciel gris de chaleur la Sphère rose et chère.
>
> Purer than a gold coin, warm yellow eyelid
> the marsh-marigold—your conjugal faith, O Spouse!—
> at noon sharp, from its tarnished mirror, envies
> in the hot grey sky the bright beloved Orb.

Morning becomes late afternoon, the sky is grey; the river seems to pursue the setting sun. But there is another drama here. The first line can be read as an evocation of the female genitalia, once intact ("Plus pure qu'un louis"); as such, it recalls the "pucelle" of the first stanza, but here (taking the part for the whole) she is "l'Epouse," a married woman. Following a lead from Hackett, who sees images of flowers as suggestive of the female genitals (Hackett, 129–30), I read the "souci d'eau" as another synecdochal representation of "l'Epouse." I believe that Collot is correct in finding here an echo of the primal scene, for all children are curious about the sexuality of their parents;[10] still it is not conjugal love that dominates but rather its opposite, jealousy. The marsh marigold ("le souci d'eau") is intermediary in the triadic series "louis—souci d'eau—foi conjugale"; its verb is "jalouse," used transitively. Under a tarnished sky she is jealous of the sun, "la Sphère rose et chère." The marriage to Captain Frédéric Rimbaud had begun well enough. "He was a tall good looking man . . . " writes Suzanne Briet.[11] Vitalie was twenty-eight, Frédéric was forty and, not long after their marriage, received the cross of the Légion d'Honneur as commendation for his service in Algeria. Although the marriage began happily, it could not last. Briet comments: "The youngest daughter of Madame Rimbaud, Frédérique-Marie-Isabelle, is born June 1, 1860. The conjugal life of the Rimbauds is over. The Captain left never to return, and will retire to Dijon in 1864. The hardships of military life had often separated them, but wasn't there also a stringent incompatibility of temperament for which both were responsible?" (14).

Vitalie Rimbaud was an unsatisfied woman, susceptible, suspicious, jealous even of "the Sun—la Sphère rose et chère. . . . " Briet calls her "authoritarian, imperious, abusive" (14). "Small, strongly built, fierce-looking, dressed in black or grey, she inspired fear, perhaps respect, but never friendship" (9). She is present in Arthur's earliest memories, disciplinarian of his earliest impulses. Face set in disapproval, impatient, threatening. All her children have felt her anger. She knows Frédéric and Arthur are always scheming to disobey her. All men are troublemakers. Her younger brother was a drunken lout, her husband was a better sort, but not to be trusted. Here it becomes apparent that memory is not the pure play of perception. It is directed along predetermined lines. Living figures populate the landscape, taking on the coloration of the unconscious. The background (upon which the specific figures have begun to emerge) is a composite: the women bathing, Vitalie and Isabelle reading books bound in red leather. All except the poet are unaware of the awesome drama that is about to occur:

> Hélas, Lui, comme
> mille anges blancs qui se séparent sur la route,
> s'éloigne par delà la montagne! Elle, toute
> froide et noire, court! après le départ de l'homme!
>
> Alas, he, like
> a thousand white angels who disperse down the road,
> vanishes beyond the mountain! She, all
> cold and dark, runs! after the departing man!

Arthur remembers the vehemence of "la mother's" anger at the time of his escape to Paris in August 1870. His own flight merges with the repeated departures of his father and takes on a mythical nimbus (mille anges blancs) in the process. "Elle, toute froide et noire; Lui, comme mille anges blancs . . . "

Again, Suzanne Briet:

> Conventional, even though brought up at the height of Romanticism, she [Mme Rimbaud] led a blameless life. She never betrayed her rigorous principles or her character. She was strong-willed, allowing her to vanquish every obstacle throughout her "sad life," which in the end even dominated Arthur. She had the misfortune to be abandoned by her husband and the sorrow to lose three children. As a recent member of the rural bourgeoisie, the sense of respectability was strong in her along with scorn of the opinion of others. A strange amalgam. . . . Work, money, religion formed the framework of her personality. Her faith was unshakeable and . . . inclined toward Jansenism. (8)

SPLITTING, which is the central feature of "Mémoire," is most pronounced in the roles attributed to "Elle," the main figure in Rimbaud's psychic life. In Part I she appears immense as she makes the entire valley her bedroom ("ayant le Ciel bleu pour ciel-de-lit"). In Part II she changes from virgin Maid to jealous spouse. Realistically drawn in Part III, with her straight back and threatening umbrella, she disciplines the weeds; then loses her dignity as, like Hera after philandering Zeus, she pursues the sun. In Part IV this comic figure is endowed with pathos: "Regret des bras épais et jeunes d'herbe pure! / Or des lunes d'avril au coeur du saint lit! Joie / des chantiers riverains à l'abandon . . . " / "Regret for the thick young arms of pure grass! / Gold of April moons deep in the holy bed! Joy / of abandoned boatyards. . . . " These lines reveal that, just as the images that represent the mother who dominates his psychic life are split, so too are the impulses toward her—reverence in the *"pucelle"* image, mockery when she wields her umbrella as rigid disciplinarian, then tenderness again when he feels sorrow for her lost love.

THE SECOND stanza of Part IV is transitional. There's a hint of impatience in the imperative of the first line of the second stanza: "Qu'elle pleure à présent sous les ramparts! / Let her weep now under the ramparts!" She cries a river, what a bore! Young Vitalie wrote in her journal in 1874: "Maman is so sad . . . I think about Arthur, his sadness, and Maman who weeps . . . " (Pléiade, 946). The poet refuses to tolerate her sorrow; there is a sharp shift of perspective: "Puis, c'est la nappe, sans reflets, sans source, grise: /—un vieux, dragueur, dans sa barque immobile, peine" / "Then, it's the surface, matte, no springs, grey: /—an old dredger, toiling in his motionless boat." The old dredger, raking the bottom for sand, enters the scene as an image of immobility.

IN PART V we have a movement similar to the "dissolve" that appears at the end of "Le Bateau ivre." Delahaye has written about the old rowboat anchored on the Meuse, where Frédéric and Arthur liked to play, pretending as they rocked from side to side that the leaky scow was carrying them on daring voyages. Here, the focus of the poem is the speaker himself; the conjugal drama is played out. The family members are gone, he is alone like the old dredger who becomes mythical—a figure of wasted time and of blighted hope.

> Jouet de cet oeil d'eau morne, je n'y puis prendre
> ô canot immobile! oh! bras trop courts! ni l'une
> ni l'autre fleur: ni la jaune qui m'importune,
> là; ni la bleue, amie à l'eau couleur de cendre.
>
> Ah! la poudre des saules qu'une aile secoue!
> Les roses des roseaux dès longtemps dévorées!
> Mon canot, toujours fixe; et sa chaîne tirée
> Au fond de cet oeil d'eau sans bords,—à quelle boue?

Chapter 4. Figures of Desire in "Mémoire"

> Toy of this eye of mournful water, I cannot pluck
> O motionless boat! O arms too short! neither this
> nor the other flower: not the yellow that entreats me,
> there; nor the blue, friend to the ashen water.
>
> Ah! dust of the willows shaken by a wing!
> The reed-roses long since withered!
> My boat, still attached; and its chain caught
> Deep in this rimless eye of water—in what mud?

His arms are too short to reach either flower. The yellow that summons him might be associated with marriage; the blue flower is ashen, colorless as the water, the color of his mother's eyes.[12] Bonnefoy reads this inability to pluck either flower as Rimbaud's sexual dilemma, his knowledge that the choice of a lover is determined by some fatality that has been imposed on him and that he cannot change. Sexual object choice is always a mystery, but in Rimbaud's case it appears to follow the classic Freudian pattern, deriving from primary narcissism. Laplanche and Pontalis write: " . . . the object is chosen on the model of the little child or adolescent that the subject once was, while the subject identifies with the mother who used to take care of him."[13] This is spelled out further by Socarides: "In the earliest phase of their childhood, future inverts pass through a period of very intense but short-lived fixation on a woman, usually their mother; after leaving this behind they identify themselves with the woman and take themselves as a sexual object. They proceed from a narcissistic basis and look for a man who resembles themselves and whom they may love as their mother loved them."[14] The true measure of Vitalie Rimbaud's power over her son lies in his unconscious identification with her. Despite all his fugues and all his complaints, he was tied to his mother by the unbreakable bond of mimetic desire.

THE POEM turns on the despairing phrase "Mon canot toujours fixe . . . / My boat forever anchored. . . . " Memory, which begins as the seemingly free play of perception, reveals its link to instinctual drives. The entire last stanza expresses Rimbaud's sadness: the buds of the water lilies are already withered; there are still many years of life ahead of him (cet oeil d'eau sans bords), but his destiny (sa chaîne) is fixed in a way that fills him with apprehension (à quelle boue?).

Years later, in Africa, Rimbaud cohabited with a woman. He treated her with respect and consideration. When finally he sent her back to her people it was with a sigh of relief and the remark, "Quelle mascarade! / What a masquerade!" But he always dreamed of marriage, if not to a bourgeoise from the Ardennes, then to a high-born black woman. He shared his dream of having a son with Isabelle. But his destiny had been determined many years earlier, by the absence of his father and the dominant character of his mother. Early on it was engraved in his instincts, his deepest desires, his "mémoire."

III

"It is this present age that has failed!"

5

What Happened in Babylone?

"Le Coeur du pitre";
Survival of the Object in "Qu'est-ce pour nous, mon coeur . . . ?"

1. "Le Coeur du pitre"

There are two great mysteries in Rimbaud's biography.[1] The first of these is his reputed enlistment in the Commune and his sojourn in the Babylone barracks, where he may have been victim of a sexual attack. The primary source is a letter from Delahaye to Verlaine, who, in 1887, was gathering material for a book on Rimbaud. In this chapter I have, by and large, followed the interpretation of Jean-Jacques Lefrère, who has abundantly documented Rimbaud's adventures in the pivotal year of 1871. Although Lefrère does not positively affirm the hypothetical gang rape of Rimbaud at Babylone, he does give a vivid (though fictive) depiction of it by Colonel Godchot, who knew all there was to know about barracks life.[2] This was Rimbaud's fourth escape from Charleville, following the third in February 1871. The first, in August 1870, ended with his arrest at the Gare du Nord (no ticket) and his confinement in the Mazas prison. The second in October 1870 took him to Douai, where he was welcomed by the Gindre sisters, aunts of his teacher, Izambard. His goal in the trips to Paris was to meet the poets of the Parnassian movement, whom he had been reading, memorizing, and imitating.

His motive for the third escape was different—the college was going to reopen and *la mother* had given him an ultimatum: either go back to school or find a job. He left sometime around April 17 and returned to

Charleville around May 13. In the capital Rimbaud met a sense of moral deterioration that he found appalling. He instinctively shared the popular hatred for the Government of National Defense that was soon to capitulate to the Germans.

A SERIES of decisive events had led up to the declaration of the Commune on March 18. The conservative Chief Executive, Thiers, grew weary of trying to run the country with half the government in Bordeaux and the other half in Paris. He made the mistake of moving the entire government to Versailles, a place with fatal monarchist associations. The Parisian National Guard, now swelled to 300,000 men, created a Federation of radical delegates who, increasingly, assumed authority. On February 28, the so-called "army of Paris" united for action and was, very soon after, ranged against the government. Edward Mason writes that the primary motive of the communards was revenge for France's defeat by Germany: "The Commune was a revolution against the 'capitulards' (the capitulators) of Bordeaux and Versailles. All the radical groups of Paris, the Blanquists, the Proudhonists, the Jacobins, and the members of the International were chauvinist in their attitude. Their opposition was directed against the supposed military weakness and the executive incapacity of the war leaders of France. Without the defeat, there would have been no Commune."[3]

IF DELAHAYE'S account of a fourth escape is to be believed (and Lefrère sees no reason to consider it a fabrication), Rimbaud left for Paris around April 19, hitchhiking and walking by turns. He arrived on or around April 23 and was stopped at the city gates, where the soldiers took up a collection for him (21 francs), and sent him off to the National Guard barracks on rue de Babylone. There he was attached to a volunteer group of *franc-tireurs* or "freedom fighters." Petitfils writes: "Paris bristled with barricades, and was plastered with white posters issuing brief orders. . . . Frightening disorder reigned in the barracks: soldiers from various regiments that had been dissolved . . . national guards, sailors, *zouaves* [indigenous Algerians serving as light infantry]—All were thrown together pell-mell" (82). During this period Rimbaud continued writing poetry, notably "Chant de guerre parisien" and a famous but enigmatic poem written in the musical form of the triolet:[4]

Le Coeur du pitre[5]

Mon triste coeur bave à la poupe,
Mon coeur est plein de caporal:
Ils y lancent des jets de soupe,
Mon triste coeur bave à la poupe:
Sous les quolibets de la troupe,
Qui pousse un rire général,
Mon triste coeur bave à la poupe,
Mon coeur couvert de caporal!

Ithyphalliques et pioupiesques
Leurs insultes l'ont dépravé!
A la vesprée, ils font des fresques
Ithyphalliques et pioupiesques.
O flots abracadabrantesques
Prenez mon coeur, qu'il soit sauvé:
Ithyphalliques et pioupiesques
Leurs quolibets l'ont depravé!

Quand ils auront tari leurs chiques
Comment agir, ô coeur volé?
Ce seront des refrains bachiques
Quand ils auront tari leurs chiques:
J'aurai des sursauts stomachiques
Si mon coeur triste est ravalé:
Quand ils auront tari leur chiques
Comment agir, ô coeur volé?
Mai 1871

The Clown's Heart

My sad heart slobbers on the poop,
My heart covered with wads of chaw:
They splatter it with jets of soup,
My sad heart slobbers on the poop:
Taking the insults of the troop
Who crack up and laugh at it,
My sad heart drools on the poop,

My heart is covered with streams of spit!

Soldier boys with swollen cocks,
Their insults have raped my heart!
When evening comes, they pantomime[6]
Soldier boys with swollen cocks.
O waves abracadabrantesques,
Take my heart and wash it clean:
Soldier boys with swollen cocks
Their wisecracks have depraved my heart!

When they will have spit their wads,
How react, O stolen heart?
There will be Bacchic burps
When they will have spit their wads:
I'll have heaves deep in my gut,
When they will have spit their wads
How react, O stolen heart?
May 1871

Antoine Adam in la Pléiade edition interprets this poem as an expression of disgust at finding himself in a barracks, surrounded by foul-mouthed, drunken men. Rimbaud had dreamed of action and adventure, but encounters instead disillusionment with the obscene behavior of the troops. The disgust is extended beyond this barracks room to the world and he calls for the sea waves to wash him clean.

Still, Rimbaud knew that poetry could be an instrument of social change. The responsibility he felt during the Commune was apparent in his draft of a constitution (known only through the testimony of his friend, Ernest Delahaye) and his reckless pronouncements at that time; but he never put his genius in the service of freedom. The brutality and obscenity of Babylone, which may have involved sodomy, cooled his "social illuminism," as Guyaux calls it. Frustration of those impulses was again part of the price he paid for being Rimbaud. Fortunately, he escaped from Babylone and headed back to Charleville, walking and hitchhiking, as he had come. He reached home in early May. Izambard, to whom he sent the poem, wrote a parody of it, wounding Rimbaud to the quick; he was careful not to display his vulnerability again.

II. Survival of the object in "Qu'est-ce pour nous, mon coeur . . . ?"

This poem begins with militant fervor and keeps building, until the emotion is disproportionate, ending in a frenzy. It is Rimbaud's version of the "Ça ira!" the revolutionary song that was hurled at the aristocrats as they rode in the tumbril on their way to the guillotine:

> Qu'est-ce pour nous, mon coeur, que les nappes de sang
> Et de braise, et mille meurtres, et les longs cris
> De rage, sanglots de tout enfer renversant
> Tout ordre; et l'Aquilon encor sur les débris . . .
>
> What's it to us, my heart, if the sheets of blood
> And of coals, and a thousand murders, and the long cries
> Of rage, sobs of all hell, reversing
> All order; and the Eagle still on the debris . . .

The manuscript is not dated, but it seems likely that the poem was written in protest against the *Semaine sanglante* (May 21–28, 1871), when thousands of Communards were executed by government troops, *les Versaillais*. Hundreds of the latter also died in the fighting. This is one of the poems that caused Rimbaud to be acclaimed "the poet of the Commune," but there is a nightmarish nihilism to the poem that suggests the infiltration of primary process into "les tourbillons de feux furieux," rather than straightforward political protest. Here, an essay by D. W. Winnicott will help to clarify the unconscious motivation that drives the imagery, and from which the poet wakes bewildered at the end of his hysterical tirade. Winnicott writes:

> . . . one of the integrating phenomena in development is the fusion of what I will here allow myself to call life and death instincts (love and strife: Empedocles). . . . This is what turns up in the baby by natural maturational process. . . .
>
> The drive is potentially 'destructive' but whether it *is* destructive or not depends on what the object is like; does the object *survive,* that is, does it retain its character, or does it *react?* If the former, then there is no destruction, or not much, and there is a next moment when the baby

can become and does gradually become aware of . . . the *fantasy* of having destroyed, hurt, damaged or provoked the object. The baby in this extreme environmental provision goes on in a pattern of developing personal aggressiveness that provides the backcloth of a continuous (unconscious) fantasy of destruction. Here we may use [Melanie] Klein's reparation concept, which links constructive play and work with this (unconscious) *fantasy backcloth* of destruction or provocation. . . . The baby at the other extreme that meets a pattern of environmental reaction or retaliation goes forward in quite a different way. . . . (emphasis in original)[7]

The baby that suffers retaliation can never return reparation for his or her own violence and is trapped by it. Earlier in this same article, Winnicott speaks about the role of the father in forging the child's sense of reality. He states that the baby makes use of the father "as a blueprint for his or her own integration. . . . If the father is not there the baby must make the same development but more arduously, or using some other fairly stable relationship to a whole person. In this way one can see that the father can be the first glimpse for the child of integration and of personal wholeness" (Winnicott, 243).

Rimbaud, without a stable father figure, would have been the second kind of baby described by Winnicott, the one whose fantasies of destruction (destrudo) never come to fruition and, therefore, are never realistically tested by his environment. We have only to think of "Après le déluge" or of "Conte." In both those poems, fantasies of destruction expand exponentially; though expressed with a different tonality and a different articulation than in "Qu'est-ce pour nous, mon coeur . . . ?" they too are never tested by reality. Of special relevance for this poem is Winnicott's reference to the Love-Strife principle, a drive that is inherent in the child at birth and that it must learn to negotiate (Winnicott writes "integrate") in its first years of life. If the "object" retains its character (i.e., if the parent responds lovingly, even when the infant is provocative), then the child will introject its love-strife tendency, retaining it as an unconscious fantasy toward the "libidinised object." By this analysis, Rimbaud is caught in between; the poem fantasizes violence, taking it as true violence, for which he must pay a price; yet at the end, he asks, "Do I wake or sleep?"

THE TURBULENCE of the unresolved oedipal triad of the child and his parents arises (following Winnicott) from the Love-Strife antithesis of

Empedocles, referred to above. Rimbaud never forgot one violent quarrel between his parents when he was six years old. To emphasize his anger, Rimbaud père grabbed a silver bowl from the sideboard and smashed it against the floor. Then, regretting his anger, he picked it up and carefully put it back in place. Whereupon Vitalie seized the bowl, raised it aloft and hurled it down with equal force. A sterling silver bowl, mind you! She too put it carefully back in its consecrated place. Such outbursts were common in the Rimbaud household. Critic Charles D. Minahen finds the poetic equivalent of this parental duel in the "vortical movement" or "turbulence" of "Qu'est-ce pour nous, mon coeur . . . ?"[8] Winnicott explains this explosive behavior in infantile experience, by the way that objects are—or are not—assimilated into imagination. In Winnicott's view it is the push-pull of powerful emotions that sets off these "tourbillons de feux furieux / whirlwinds of furious fire," which introduce an internal space or geometry into this highly self-reflexive poem. Minahen's book *Vortex/t*, in which the revised essay on Rimbaud was later published,[9] makes a unique contribution to our understanding of both Rimbaud and Mallarmé, by demonstrating the production of three-dimensional spaces within the linearity of the poems.

The poem ends with the poet's seeming to wake from a dream: "Ce n'est rien! j'y suis! j'y suis toujours" ("It's nothing! I'm here, I'm still here!"). In his poetic fantasy he dreamed the world destroyed, all order broken, the very continents sucked into the maelstrom: "Europe, Asie, Amérique, disparaissez / Europe, Asia, America, disappear."

The poet, who will later write "Et pas une main d'ami; et où puiser le secours?" ("And not even a friendly hand; and where turn for help?"), dreams of the camaraderie of men at arms, fighting in a desperate cause:

Oh! mes amis!—Mon coeur, c'est sûr, ils sont des frères:
Noirs inconnus, si nous allions! allons! allons!
O malheur! je me sens frémir, la vieille terre,
Sur moi de plus en plus à vous! la terre fond . . .

Oh! my friends—My heart, tells me, they are brothers:
Unknown blacks, what say we leave! Come! Come!
O misery! I feel myself tremble, this old earth,
Melts around me, I'm more and more yours . . .

Yet on his return to reality, after this emotional paroxysm, he finds that nothing has changed: like the silver bowl, the objects of his destructive passion have survived. A tragic bewilderment is implicit in the last line, "Ce n'est rien! j'y suis! j'y suis toujours." This recalls the end of "Mémoire," where the "bras trop courts / arms too short" encounter another aspect of his characterological destiny.

To summarize the view of Rimbaud that Winnicott's paradigm gives us, we can say that the destructive impulse, or destrudo, is incompletely fantasized, probably because of the father's absence. As a result, the child is caught between action and inaction, between fantasy and deed. These two poems illustrate Rimbaud's deep emotional involvement with the Commune and his paralysis when confronted with an instinctive imperative for action. Whether out of good sense or panic, he avoided any deeper involvement with the Commune; but he hadn't yet finished writing about that traumatic episode in his country's history.

6

Synchronicity

"A Une Raison"; "Démocratie"

1. "A Une Raison"

"A Une Raison / To A Reason" is one of the *Illuminations,* probably an early one. It stages Rimbaud's effort to present his political vision. From a broader perspective it represents a poetic statement of the Continental rationalism that reigned from Descartes to Leibnitz. Rationalism proclaims that reason is the unique path to knowledge and right action. The Continental rationalists (in opposition to the British empiricists—Locke, Berkeley, Hume) believed that reason penetrates directly to the essence of things. In "A Une Raison" Rimbaud borrows the rationalistic aspirations of various splinter groups of the Commune, for example, the "Hébertists," a radical fringe movement:

> The coming of the Hébertists was the advent of science and of reason in its most energetic and popular form, the form which alone could assure a definitive triumph. The science of the Girondins, of the doctrinaires, was cloistered in a lettered oligarchy; was drawn from the boudoir and exhibited in the market place. The Hébertists addressed themselves to the people and said, "Science is your conquest, science belongs to you, come and take it." (Mason, 13, n18)

A Une Raison

Un coup de ton doigt sur le tambour décharge tous les sons et
    commence la nouvelle harmonie.
Un pas de toi, c'est la levée des nouveaux hommes et leur en-marche.
Ta tête se détourne,—le nouvel amour!
Ta tête se retourne,—le nouvel amour!
"Change nos lots, crible les fléaux, à commencer par le temps," te
    chantent ces enfants. "Elève n'importe où la substance de nos
    fortunes et de nos voeux" on t'en prie.
Arrivée de toujours, qui t'en iras partout.

A tap of your finger on the drum releases all sounds and begins the new
    harmony.
You take one step, and it's the rising of the new men and their forward
    march.
Your head turns to one side,—new love!
Your head turns to the other,—new love!
The children sing: "Change our fate, wipe out the plagues, beginning
    with time." They beg you, "Increase anywhere the substance of our
    fortunes and of our prayers."
Always arriving, you depart everywhere.

Reason is a drummer boy, like those twelve-year-old orphans ("ces enfants") who drummed the *pas de charge* to send the armies of Napoleon I into battle. There is an intimacy between the poet and Reason, addressed as "tu." This intimacy becomes mimicry: each gesture orchestrates events, producing synchronicity or "la nouvelle harmonie."[1] Reason (embodied in the poet) possesses total power over humanity "en marche" toward progress:

Ta tête se détourne,—le nouvel amour![2]
Ta tête se retourne,—le nouvel amour!

This poem is the drumbeat of rationalism in the service of right action, a use of cognition that attracted Rimbaud, despite the deep currents of irrationality that stirred so powerfully in him and inspired his greatest poetry.

The rationality of this poem is primarily political, since the proposed use of reason leads to "des nouveaux hommes / new men" and their "nouvel amour / new love." Reason is the faculty in us that connects us to an order of things in the universe, which itself can be called rational. Mind and world coincide; thought and event become synchronous. Reason, the poem tells us, guides us to action in the service of mankind.

BUT DOES "A Une Raison" truly offer us a world? This poem was written in 1872 or '73, around the time of the disillusionment of *Une Saison en enfer.* Rimbaud still wants to believe that a new kind of love will emerge from the chaos of events. But he reduces it to a mere reflex rather than a powerfully motivated act: "Ta tête se détourne: le nouvel amour." Even the use of a favorite metaphor for health and happiness—music—fails to inflate this poem, to lift it above the ground and set it free. There is a certain poignancy in the singing children, who ask the impossible; one might even hear the children of Africa, asking for the end of typhus and malaria ("crible les fléaux") or for a chance, any chance at all to have a decent life: "Elève n'importe où la substance de nos fortunes et de nos voeux. . . . "

The poem calls for a hero, awaited by children, by lovers, by suffering mankind. In the hero's presence we all act as one, our words and gestures are synchronized, together we march out of *always* into *everywhere.* The psychic procedure here tilts between embodied intelligence, where the thinking agent is embedded in a culture, and depersonalization, where the relation of mind to world is given in the dualism of a strict rational science. It is the latter that prevails in this truncated poem.

One can't help but feel that the violence and brutality associated with the Commune destroyed the vibrant political energy Rimbaud had once possessed. He needs to distance himself from the Commune, even while he celebrates it. "A Une Raison" does not have the passionate character of earlier poems written to celebrate the Commune or to decry the terrible massacre that ended it; instead it is chillingly impersonal. It is foreshortened, bitten off like an expletive.

The last line ("Arrivée de toujours, qui t'en iras partout") makes a grandiose prediction. André Guyaux explains: "The last sentence insists on the atemporality and the universality of that Reason: It has always been necessary, and it will propagate itself *everywhere,* in all places" (*Oeuvres,* 540). Yet this ubiquitous Reason distances the speaker from the here and now of his engagement. Rationalism is a mode of thinking that discounts our worldly embodiment, substituting a mechanical model for the plasticity of our bodily and cultural reality. In "A Une Raison" the poet's speech is far more mechanical than it is informal or free.

Along with a dose of enthusiasm, we get a sense here of the disenchantment involved in Rimbaud's career. His early successes were accompanied by denunciations both of himself and of his poetry. His checkered rise to fame coincided with a chaotic period in French history. He hoped that the rise of "Reason" would bring not only social progress but his own vindication as a man. Instead, he was assaulted in the Babylone barracks and a savage massacre ended the Commune. *La Semaine sanglante* (Week of Blood), in which more than fifteen thousand individuals were executed,[3] must have seemed like the metaphor for his own dreams and desires. Only a few of his poems were in print; the publication of *Une Saison en enfer* passed unnoticed. Finally, there was the tragedy of Verlaine and his imprisonment. "A Une Raison" seems to mark—inauspiciously—the midpoint in the rise and fall of Rimbaud's career.

II. Critic or Accomplice? "Démocratie"

'Le drapeau va au paysage immonde, et notre patois étouffe le tambour.
'Aux centres nous alimenterons la plus cynique prostitution. Nous massacrerons les révoltes logiques.
'Aux pays poivrés et détrempés!—au service des plus monstrueuses exploitations industrielles ou militaires.
'Au revoir ici, n'importe où. Conscrits du bon vouloir, nous aurons la philosophie féroce; ignorants pour la science, roués pour le confort; la crevaison pour le monde qui va. C'est la vraie marche. En avant, route!'

"The flag moves through a filthy landscape, and our patois drowns out the drum.
"In the interior, we'll feed the most cynical whoring. We'll massacre all reasonable revolts.
"To the sodden lands of spices!—in service to the most monstrous industrial or military exploitation.
"Farewell to here, anywhere else will do. We willing conscripts have a ferocious philosophy; ignorant of science, used to comfort; and let the world explode. This is the true way forward. Double time, march!"

Antoine Adam suggests that Rimbaud wrote this poem after May 1876, when he enlisted in the Dutch infantry, embarked for Java in July, and then deserted, returning to France. Bernard and Guyaux, however, are reluctant to believe that Rimbaud was still writing poetry at that time. No manuscript of the poem exists, adding to the difficulty of interpretation. In his critical edition of the *Illuminations,* André Guyaux gives a rhetorical analysis of this poem that sheds light on the effect of "mise en abyme," produced by the quotation marks and the ambiguity arising from the fact that poet and fictive speaker are both distinct and the same.[4] Guyaux seems to be saying that what is, on one level, a "political pamphlet" is, on another, a cynical eulogy, in fact a critique, of the exploitation of Third World countries by "democratic" armies. Rimbaud may well be indicting the invasion and colonization of Algeria by Napoleon III.

Kristin Ross adds a useful comment in her study of Rimbaud and the Paris Commune:

> The term "démocratie" undergoes a profound modification during the Second Empire when it is appropriated by the imperial regime in opposition to the bourgeois regime—the emperor claiming to have given back to the people its sovereignty. . . . Republicans and Socialists hesitated to use such a tainted word: Blanqui, for example, in 1852 writes, "Qu'est-ce qu'un démocrate, je vous prie? C'est un mot vague, banal, sans acception précise, un mot en caoutchouc." ("What is a democrat, I ask you? It is a vague and banal word, one without any precise meaning, a rubber word.") Rimbaud plays with the ideological slippage of the term when he entitles his parody of colonial discourse "Democracy."[5]

Reading this poem today, in the context of contemporary events, I find that it makes perfect sense. It satirizes the motives of democracies that put down "les révoltes logiques," ravage the resources of Third World countries (" . . . au service des plus monstrueuses exploitations industrielles ou militaires"), all in the name of maintaining "le confort" of their way of life. Its ambiguity perfectly expresses the uneasy conscience of ordinary citizens, who help support the "Conscrits du bon vouloir," sent on missions that are ill defined by politicians "ignorants pour la science."

Rimbaud heard the term "democracy" bandied about in the barracks on the Rue de Babylone, but he had confronted the issue of inequality long before that. He had his first lessons in "democracy" at the age of seven, when he played with the neighborhood children, all from poor families, not up to the standard of Mme Rimbaud, who caught her son engaging in sexual play ("des pitiés immondes / in dirty games") with an eight-year-old ("La petite brutale / The little brute"). She never wore panties and he bit her ass. Babylone brought a brutality of a different order; there, he was the one with the bloody backside.

In spite of many disillusionments, Rimbaud maintained his political liberalism even in Africa, where he learned the native languages, mingled with the people, and was an exponent of liberty, equality, and fraternity. The anger and defiance that he'd learned in his childhood were alive and well until the very end. He was never a trader in slaves, but the blacks who staffed his caravans were indentured men rented out by avaricious chiefs. He is reputed to have treated them well, but he must have known (and bitterly resented) his complicity in the caravanning that was the principal business of the white traders in Abyssinia. His failed attempt to reward his beloved servant, Djami, when he lay dying in the Hôpital de la Conception in Marseilles was a final irony in this short life (Rimbaud died at the age of thirty-seven), made up of disappointment and contradiction. Djami himself had already died by the time the inheritance reached his family.

IV

"...the most intense music"

7

The Child as Thaumaturge

"Après le déluge"

"Après le déluge" is about magic, about the power of childhood, about what Freud called "the omnipotence of thoughts, a belief in the thaumaturgic force of words."[1] It has little to do with any grievances Rimbaud may have felt, but rather the power of childhood wishes and the knowledge in the young narcissist's heart that he has power to change the world.

This is traditionally the first of the *Illuminations,* by convention rather than any certainty based on the autograph (by Verlaine) or on hard evidence. Since it is on a separate page of the manuscript, André Guyaux places it together with the other *Illuminations* that are impossible to collate with accuracy.

Rimbaud begins with the adverb "Aussitôt / As soon as," suggesting the immediacy that characterizes "Après le déluge." It's a poem about making things happen by wanting them, a power reserved to dictators, magicians, and children, which is why it is the *idea* of the flood that subsides before everything starts over again: this momentous restoration of the world happens in the mind of a child.

Some critics have seen "Après le déluge" as an allegory of the Commune and its bloody repression. This is suggested by an article quoted in the Pléiade edition:

> When the immense hope of the Commune subsided, the bourgeois, timid as a rabbit, takes over again. He gives thanks to God (the rainbow) for having saved him in religious rituals (the spider-web).... (Pléiade, 798)

Albert Henry improves on this simplistic interpretation by recognizing a double meaning in the title "Après le déluge" that indicates a time both biblical and contemporaneous. He comments that "After the Flood" contains "the theme of the Biblical Flood through picturesque details found in the rebirth of nature"; but Henry also sees here the "Flood" of the Commune.[2] I find this interpretation far-fetched; the spontaneity and freshness of "Après le déluge" distinguish it from any of the political poems, such as "Le Mal" or "Chant de Guerre parisien." or "Qu'est-ce pour nous mon coeur...?" There is no hint of an *arrière-pensée* (double meaning) or of the creaky articulation associated with allegory.

LET'S TAKE the poem at face value. You can picture it in your mind's eye. Children are sitting in the parlor reading a book of Bible stories containing colored pictures. They are "en deuil / in mourning" because it is raining outside and they can't play. This adjectival phrase, "en deuil," is an important clue to the psychic mechanism central to the poem's action. Children are hyperbolic beings: a rainy day is worse than a death in the family.

Here we see Rimbaud as animist, displaying his belief that nature is inhabited by spirits. A hare says its prayer to the rainbow, jewels hide in the earth. It's happening so fast you almost miss the flowers looking around (implied by the adverb "déjà / already"). This animistic quality, literal for the child-protagonist, is seen by some critics as a display of artifice, a "magic-lantern show," or as Sergio Sacchi puts it: "... from a certain point of view 'Après le déluge' is no more than a series of illustrations, of vignettes, of brief tableaux, of figurines, of icons ... in short, Rimbaud is experimenting with a whole range of different techniques of representation" (Sacchi, 44). But this reading, as a display of poetic virtuosity, distracts us from the child's-eye viewpoint that is central to the poem.

The poem has opened *in medias res*. We must reach the line that starts "Dans la grande maison.../ In the big house..." before Rimbaud draws a frame around the action that's already begun. We hear a door slam, a child stands in the village square twirling his arms, a classic protest against boredom. This boy, with his short pants and knobby knees, is a thaumaturge, possessed of magical powers. The church-towers and weathervanes understand that he can work miracles.

It is a miracle of destruction, begun while he ("l'enfant de colère / the child born of anger," as Rimbaud has been called) was in the parlor, reading about the Flood. He calls on free-floating fantasies of destruction, enshrined inside him since before he was born. Melanie Klein offers this amazing insight as a fundamental axiom of her practice:

> In attacking its mother's inside . . . the child is attacking a great number of objects, and is embarking on a course which is fraught with consequences. The womb first stands for the world; and the child originally approaches this world with desires to attack and destroy it, and is therefore prepared from the outset to view the real, external world as more or less hostile to itself, and peopled with objects ready to make attacks upon it. Its belief that in thus attacking its mother's body it has also attacked its father and its brothers and sisters, and, in a wider sense the whole world, is, in my experience, one of the underlying causes of its sense of guilt, and of the development of its social and moral feelings in general.[3]

If we accept this theory of universal infantile destructiveness, which is akin to the notion of original sin, it accounts for the déluge which *precedes* the start of the poem; but what about the consequent guilt?[4] Is that the motive for the rapid resurrection of civilization? There is no evidence of guilt in the brief notations, like stage directions in a play, that accompany the rebuilding of the world:

> Dans la grande rue sale les étals se dressèrent, et l'on tira les barques vers la mer étagée là-haut comme sur les gravures.
> Le sang coula, chez Barbe-Bleue,—aux abbatoirs,—dans les cirques, où le sceau de Dieu blêmit les fenêtres. Le sang et le lait coulèrent.
> Les castors bâtirent. Les "mazagrans" fumèrent dans les estaminets.[5]

> In the filthy main street stalls were erected, and boats were hauled toward the sea situated up above as in engravings.
> Blood flowed at Bluebeard's,—in slaughter-houses,—in circuses, wherever God's seal blemished the windows. Blood and milk flowed.
> Beavers built. Glasses of black coffee steamed in the cafes.

These are mere statements of fact with no emotional quotient (such as guilt); or, to use another analogy, they are like quick notations in a painting. We remember that Verlaine, in his preface to the 1886 edition of the *Illuminations,* explained the title as a reference to "gravures coloriées / colored plates."[6] The poet is an artist whose rapid brushstrokes design the fall and rise of a civilization, albeit a pretentious one (the piano in the Alps).

RESONATING powerfully against the poet's rapid notations is the Book of Genesis, known to any mindful nineteenth-century reader. Indeed, Rimbaud's poem might well be seen as sacrilegious by someone overly pious, like his mother, who genuflected twenty times a day before a statue of Our Lady in the farmhouse in Roche.

In his comparison of "Après le déluge" with the Book of Genesis, Lawler emphasizes the poem's form: "Verse paragraphs, the gravely committed diction, the syntax, the Flood imagery require us to give weight to a ritual poem" (130). The "verse paragraphs" (les versets) are the passages, rarely more than two lines in length, that form a unified whole and can be spoken aloud in one breath. They are an innovation that Rimbaud brought to the prose poem and that became the preferred verse pattern for Paul Claudel. I take Lawler's phrase "gravely committed" as referring to a certain sobriety in the enumeration of events, a lack of adjectival ornamentation. Lawler sees the poem as a direct contradiction of Genesis. This is a plausible reading; but I think it is secondary to the ludic reading that I find dominant. The child-poet has a new toy; he can turn creation off and on, on and off. He builds a castle of blocks, then knocks it down, only to build it up again. The world that appears with its caravans and its Splendide Hotel blazing in the Alps is a miniaturized world.

Some critics give metaphysical weight to the child-poet's destructiveness. Yves Bonnefoy believes that "Après le déluge" was written during a period of sadness and a consequent "spirit of negation" during the autumn of 1873 in London. He sees here "the revolt, the violent denial of all order announced in the *Lettre du voyant,* and evoked again in the prologue of *Une Saison*" (150). For Bonnefoy the Sorceress, with her "clay pot," represents the hallucinatory world of hashish, a frequent indulgence in London. Bonnefoy's way of reading the poem parallels the concept of infantile aggression as theorized by Melanie Klein; but, in my opinion, it violates the reverential spirit of "Après le déluge," conveyed by the biblical repetitions in the first part of the poem ("sur la terre," "sous le ciel," "l'eau du déluge"). This awed enumeration is followed, as Lawler shows, by "a quasi-refrain and phonetic iteration such as the twenty occurrences of open *e* followed by *r*, which becomes the groundnote that gives accumulative basis to the intrusion of the 'Sorcière' at the end of the poem . . . " (132).

Violence interrupts this ritualized discourse with a series of imperatives and a choppy, accelerated rhythm: "Sourds, étang—écume, roule sur le pont et par-dessus les bois; draps noirs et orgues,—éclairs et tonnerre,— montez et roulez;—Eaux et tristesses, montez et relevez les Déluges / Surge, pond—foam, roll over the bridge and through the woods; black palls and organs, lightning and thunder,—-rise up and roll;—Waters and sorrows, rise and revive the Floods."

It is only here, in the poem's conclusion, beginning again with an adverbial phrase of temporality "Depuis lors, / Since then," that the emotional quotient increases:

> Depuis lors, la Lune entendit les chacals piaulant par les déserts de thym,—et les églogues en sabot grognant dans le verger. Puis, dans la futaie violette, bourgeonnante, Eucharis me dit que c'était le printemps.

He has called for the floods to return—Sourds, étang,—montez et roulez; Eaux et tristesses, montez et relevez les Déluges." It is his boredom, his sadness ("tristesses") that demands them. And he explains:

> Car depuis qu'ils se sont dissipés,—oh les pierres précieuses s'enfouissant, et les fleurs ouvertes!—c'est un ennui! et la Reine, la Sorcière qui allume sa braise dans le pot de terre, ne voudra jamais nous raconter ce qu'elle sait, et que nous ignorons.

> For since then, the Moon heard jackals howling in the deserts of thyme,—and eclogues in wooden shoes grumbling in the orchard. Then in the violet budding grove, Eucharis told me that it was spring.
> —Gush forth, pond,—Foam, roll on the bridge and through the woods;—Black shrouds and organs,—lightning and thunder,—rise up and roll;—Waters and sadness, mount up and restore the Floods.
> For since they have gone,—oh! the precious stones burying themselves, and the flowers opened!—what a bother! and the Queen, the Sorceress who lights her coals in her clay pot, will never tell us what she knows, and what we will never learn.

Since civilization has recovered, the world has become hostile with "jackals howling in the deserts of thyme." The phrase "eglogues en sabot" evokes peasants in wooden shoes grumbling in the orchard. And then the insipid nymph Eucharis states the obvious: Spring has sprung! The youthful thaumaturge orders Nature to rise up and erase this pretentious civilization: "Eaux et tristesses, montez et relevez les Déluges!"

Alas, Nature does not respond. The poet mimics the child protagonist by using an infantile voice: "c'est un ennui! / what a bore!"

THE SORCERESS is a borrowing from Michelet, whose book *La Sorcière* influenced Rimbaud at multiple points. As Enid Starkie observes, Rimbaud took over Michelet's view of witches, demons, and criminals (and she might have added "children") as the real creators of the Renaissance that emerged from the Middle Ages. Here, the Sorceress figures the mystery of Nature, whose conduct, though sometimes predictable (e.g., the seasons), is, in the last analysis, beyond human control. Who better than a child to consider this paradox, as he stands forlorn in the empty village square and lets himself be drenched by the "éclatante giboulée / glittering downpour"? Bonnefoy sees *La Sorcière* as a dark temptress, with hashish in her "pot de terre." Rimbaud, this lonely child, was always looking for adventure; but in this poem what he longs for is not the oblivion of absinthe or the illusions of hashish but the moment when the flower opens, the jewels shine, and time (almost) stops—in that split second between the lightning flash and the clap of thunder.

8

Abreaction in Three Poems
"Honte"; "Angoisse"; "Aube"

> Only emotion can cure emotion.
> —Spinoza

1. "Honte / Shame"

"Honte" was probably written in Charleville in spring of 1872, after Rimbaud's ignominious return from Paris, where Verlaine had been supporting him. He had caused scandal at the traditional banquet of the Parnassian group, Les Vilains Bonshommes / The Nasty Goodfellows, and was told never to return.[1] Verlaine (who would remain bisexual all his life) had briefly reconciled with his wife. So Rimbaud came home, his heart full of shame and anger. There is an obvious reference to Verlaine ("Lui") and their quarrels, when Verlaine blamed "l'enfant/Gêneur" / "the intrusive child" for breaking up his marriage. My reason for putting "Honte" here is that it is one of only three poems of Rimbaud titled with an affective word.

In this section I want to study the way Rimbaud elicits emotion and then resolves it using a kind of homeopathic process, according to which "like-cures-like."[2] Here the poet's overwhelming "Shame" is released by a second dose of shame (he stinks like a Rocky Mountain wildcat, a nonexistent beast) and an ironic turn, the prayer for God's mercy.

A large number of poems in the lyrical tradition exhibit this basic way of dealing with emotion, which will be called here by the psychoanalytic term "abreaction." Freud and Breuer developed the term to explain the cure of hysterical symptoms under hypnosis. Freud writes of the theory developed in *Studies on Hysteria*:

> ... it introduced a dynamic factor, by supposing that a symptom arises through the damming-up of an affect, and an economic factor, by regarding that same symptom as the product of the transformation of an amount of energy which would otherwise have been employed in some other way.... Breuer spoke of our method as *cathartic;* its therapeutic aim was explained as being to provide that the quota of affect used for maintaining the symptom, which had got on to the wrong lines and had, as it were, become strangulated there, should be directed on to the normal path along which it could obtain discharge (or *abreaction*).[3]

Honte

Tant que la lame n'aura
Pas coupé cette cervelle,
Ce paquet blanc vert et gras
A vapeur jamais nouvelle,

(Ah! Lui, devrait couper son
Nez, sa lèvre, ses oreilles,
Son ventre! et faire abandon
De ses jambes! ô merveille)

Mais, non, vrai, je crois que tant
Que pour sa tête la lame,
Que les cailloux pour son flanc,
Que pour ses boyaux la flamme

N'auront pas agi, l'enfant
Gêneur, la si sotte bête,
Ne doit cesser un instant
De ruser et d'être traître

Comme un chat des Monts-Rocheux;
D'empuantir toutes sphères!
Qu'à sa mort pourtant, ô mon Dieu!
S'élève quelque prière!

Shame

So long as the blade has
Not sliced that brain, that
Green-white packageful of grease
And stinking steam

(Ah! He should cut off his
Nose, his lips, his ears,
His belly! and spread
His legs! O miracle!)

But no; truly, I swear
That for his head, the blade
The stones for his side,
For his bowels, the flame,

Unless they act, the troublesome
Child, the very stupid beast,
Will never for a moment stop
His cheating and betraying,

And like a Rocky Mountain cat,
Will reek to the very spheres!
Yet at his death, O Lord,
May some prayers be said!

The conjunction "Tant que / So long as" plunges us into the death sentence Rimbaud pronounces on himself. It is gruesome and involves carving up his brain: "Ce paquet blanc vert et gras, / A vapeur jamais nouvelle. . . ." The butchery continues with the rest of his body. The short (seven-syllable), highly segmented lines give a staccato beat to this death sentence and also add a colloquial quality, as if people are gossiping. Rimbaud is the speaker but this is not his voice; he is mimicking the voices of his critics. These include Verlaine's wife, in-laws, and friends, several of whom he had insulted and one of whom he had attacked, also his mother and her circle of acquaintances.

To read the poem emotionally, we have to put ourselves in the mind of the poet as he mimics the critics of his behavior. He asks: *Is this what* you want? Will this satisfy you?* Clearly his "shame" is tinged with self-righteous indignation. The images of butchery reach their climax in the third stanza. In the fourth stanza, the clause introduced by the repetition of "Tant que" concludes the conditions that must be fulfilled before the culprit can be properly punished. The culprit's identity is emphasized by the position of "l'enfant" at the end of a line and "Gêneur" at the start of the next. This marks the pivot between guilt and punishment. And here we begin to see how shame is abreacted: first, by the evocation of a mythical beast, "un chat des Monts-Rocheux," whose stench fills the world, to make him seem less than human.[4] The irony of the comparison is heightened by the hypocritical call for prayers to save his soul in the final distich.

Irony was always Rimbaud's best instrument for turning away wrath. The double viewpoint (of speaker and imagined personae) is maintained throughout the poem, reaching its climax in the last two stanzas. Just to the degree that the punishment is excessive, to that degree the speaker feels shame and resentment; but he doesn't plead to be pardoned. When he asks for prayers in the last two lines, it is evident that his accusers are the guilty parties, those who need divine intervention to forgive their hardheartedness. It is this ironic reversal, casting shame back on his accusers (his mother? Verlaine? others who commiserated with Mme Rimbaud?) that produces abreaction.

11. "Angoisse / Anguish"

> Every scansion is as much an act of interpretation as it is of description.[5]

"Angoisse" is the second poem of Rimbaud's titled with an emotive word.[6] The poem opens with a hypothetical that begins in the first paragraph, is interrupted by a parenthesis in the second paragraph, and concludes in the third paragraph with a question mark. Here are those paragraphs, aptly described by Lawler as "surges" (176):

> Se peut-il qu'Elle me fasse pardonner les ambitions continuellement écrasées,—qu'une fin aisée répare les âges d'indigence,—qu'un jour de succès nous endorme sur la honte de notre inhabileté fatale,
> (O palmes! diamant!—Amour, force!—plus haut que toutes joies et gloires!—de toutes façons, partout,—Démon, dieu,—Jeunesse de cet être-ci; moi!)
> Que des accidents de féerie scientifique et des mouvements de frater-

nité sociale soient chéris comme restitution progressive de la franchise première? . . .

Can it be that She might allow forgiveness of my ambitions continually crushed,—that a wealthy old age might compensate my years of poverty,—that one day's success might blind us to the shame of our fatal awkwardness,

(O palms! diamonds! Love, power!–higher than all joys and glories!—of every kind, everywhere,—Demon, god—Youth of this being here and now; myself!)

Can accidents of scientific magic and movements of social brotherhood be cherished as the progressive restitution of originary freedom? . . .

Lawler notes that the poet is seeking "a possible redemption," but who is it that holds power to redeem a life; who is "Elle"? The last two paragraphs tell us more about her:

Mais la Vampire qui nous rend gentils commande que nous nous amusions avec ce qu'elle nous laisse, ou qu'autrement nous soyons plus drôles.

Rouler aux blessures, par l'air lassant et la mer; aux supplices, par le silence des eaux et de l'air meurtriers; aux tortures qui rient, dans leur silence atrocement houleux.

But the Vampire who makes us behave commands us to enjoy whatever she leaves us, or otherwise we'll end up even more laughable.

Let us roll in our wounds, through the heavy air and the sea; in our torments, through the silence of waters and the murderous air; in our tortures which jeer us, through their fiendish billowy silence.

Suzanne Bernard comments on the poem's structure: "This is one of the most disturbing poems of the *Illuminations;* we feel a lift (élan), then a fall (une retombée), anguish follows excessive hopes; but these impressions are veiled, allusive, hard to interpret" (*Oeuvres,* 565). Bernard reads "Elle" (la Vampire) as death, characterizing the poem's affectivity as a struggle with the last things. The poet asks what life holds for him, what are his chances for success after almost twenty years of indigence and failure. Will he one day be in a position to forget "la honte de notre inhabileté fatale"? Note the return of "shame," a too familiar state of mind for

Rimbaud. I think he refers to his social gaucherie: his never-to-be-forgotten arrival at the home of Verlaine's in-laws; his tongue-tied awkwardness in expressing gratitude to Izambard; his rude behavior at meetings of Les Vilains Bonshommes; his embarrassed relations with women and girls. Use of this word (*honte*/"shame") rules out any interpretation that sees his failure as involving poetic creation. Rimbaud knew well that he was not "inhabile" as a poet. Failure or success then must be read in a broader sense as "savoir vivre."

Also underlying the association of "Angoisse" with death is the fact that, as Lawler points out (181), the fourth "Spleen" of Baudelaire is the principal intertext for Rimbaud's poem. The last stanza of Baudelaire's poem reads:

> —Et de longs corbillards, sans tambours ni musique,
> Défilent lentement dans mon âme; l'Espoir,
> Vaincu, pleure, et l'Angoisse atroce, despotique,
> Sur mon crâne incliné plante son drapeau noir.

> —And long funeral convoys, without music or drums,
> Defile slowly in my soul; Hope,
> Vanquished, weeps, and atrocious Anguish, despot,
> On my bent skull plants her black banner.

Baudelaire's elegiac alexandrines are skillfully echoed by the longer prose lines of "Angoisse." A further recurrence is achieved by the abstract nouns ("Amour, force! . . . Jeunesse . . . accidents de féerie scientifique et des mouvements de fraternité sociale . . . .") that give both poems their allegorical, reverberative character.

"Angoisse" is an example of the way that Rimbaud deals with negative emotion, by calling forth and then, through rhythm and imagery, resolving or "abreacting" it. The emotion, of course, is "anguish." In the first paragraph the interrogative "Se peut-il . . . " is followed by three taps of the relative "que," expressing self-doubt tinged with bitterness. The élan of which Bernard speaks occurs in the accelerating rhythm (note the rhymes in "pardonn*er*," "écras*ées*," and "ais*ée*") and the strong tonic and secondary accents of "me *fasse* pardonner," echoed in "qu'une *fin* aisée répare les âges d'*indigence;* the "retombée" comes in the rest of the sentence, after the tonic of "*succès*," followed by the lengthening of the second syllable of "endorme" and the final double accent on "*fatale*."

The following parenthetical paragraph is composed exclusively of interjections. Palms and diamonds are rewards of the winner, love and strength are higher than joy and glory. Dislocation, occurring in the last expression ("Démon, dieux—Jeunesse de cet être-ci; moi!") places strong accentuation on the intensive pronoun, lending power to the self-affirmation that follows the self-doubting first paragraph. These features give a rhythmic lift or surge to the paragraph and project the poem into a new dimension, beginning the abreactive process.

The second paragraph then calls up "succès" by a series of invocations, providing a pivot on which the argument turns into the third stanza, here again a relative clause depending on "Se peut-il. . . . " This introjected object ("une fin aisée . . . un jour de succès") is absent for the poet and doubly absent for the reader, who must fantasize another's fantasy. Poetic emotion arises in response to the *absence* of its object. The absent object of need must be invoked within a tensional field. In the third paragraph, still doubting of his own strength, he looks for a social-historical agency: "des accidents de féerie scientifique et des mouvements de fraternité sociale . . ." The reference here is probably to Michelet's "nouvel amour" (new forms of love) and the manifestos of the revolutionary writers of 1848 and 1870. As for "féerie scientifique," Bernard sees it as a reference to electricity, a novelty of that time. Can participation in these inventions and social movements redeem him? If the Vampire is death, as I think she is, none of these shibboleths can save him.

HOW THEN does Rimbaud release or abreact the emotion that he himself has identified as anguish? By one of his most common and effective escape valves—mockery. In the fourth section, introduced by "Mais la Vampire . . . " he implicitly dismisses the appeal, in the preceding paragraph, to high-minded ideology. It was all very well for Michelet, an old man with a new wife half his age, to blather about his rebirth: "I feel myself . . . full of devotion and fervor, before these gleams of God embodied in woman."[7] The Vampire makes us behave ourselves. Rimbaud has seen the hour of Death in peasant families in the Ardennes. The hush, the tears held back, a priest administering the last rites. Death teaches us to be content with what we have ("ce qu'elle nous laisse") or otherwise we'll end up even worse off ("qu'autrement nous soyons plus drôles").

And here are the alternatives, here is the way you might conclude. Using the figure of zeugma, the infinitive-imperative "Rouler" governs three noun clauses: "aux blessures," "aux supplices," and "aux tortures."

All three have an adverbial function, showing exactly how you will "quake" as you undergo these torments. But the mockery is still there, in the oxymoronic phrases "le silence des eaux et de l'air meurtrier; aux tortures qui rient, dans leur silence atrocement houleux."

The poem has the form of a folk tale, a ghost story. It asks a serious question about death (first paragraph). In the second paragraph the teller boasts that he's equal to death—he is a demon or a god! And besides, in this modern world, progress will guarantee the rights of all of us. (Unfortunately, that doesn't include the right not to die.)

Death is a Vampire, so beware, treat Her with respect; otherwise you'll be caught in a punishing swell, your torturers will laugh in their murderous silence as you are carried past on the wave of time. When he wrote "Angoisse," Rimbaud may have remembered the state of exaltation in which he penned "Le Bateau ivre"; but those days are long gone. More likely, he remembers the terror he felt on July 9, 1873, cowering against a locked door in the Hôtel de la Ville de Courtrai, looking down the barrel of Verlaine's revolver.

III. "Aube / Dawn"

"Aube" also enacts the rise and fall of an emotion. This is one of the poems that justify speaking of animism in Rimbaud, or, more simply, of a child's sensitivity to nature. Delahaye writes that when they went on walks together: "He made me look at the trees, the sky, lit by that inexpressible light, the first hour of morning" (*Oeuvres, 559*).

The first line is frankly sensual: "J'ai embrassé l'aube d'été" ("I kissed the summer dawn"). It is this desire to possess and be possessed by nature that constitutes the emotional nexus of the poem. The second line sets a fairy tale scene: "Rien ne bougeait encore au front des palais" ("Nothing yet moved on the fronts of the palaces"). In this setting, at such a moment, anything can happen. Yet the next two sentences evoke quiescence, shadows: "L'eau était morte. Les camps d'ombres ne quittaient pas la route du bois" ("The water was deathly still. Camps of shadows still held the road through the forest"). Little by little, as the child enters the woods, emanations rise, life stirs: "J'ai marché, réveillant les haleines vives et tièdes, et les pierreries regardèrent, et les ailes se levèrent sans bruit" ("As I walked, awakening lively yet tepid breaths, the stones looked around, and wings flapped without noise"). The first line is octosyllabic, the second an alexandrine. The third line has four syllables, the following fourteen. As the next verset swells (32 syllables), life comes to the forest.

This poem is Disneyesque long before the existence of the animated cartoon. The very stones look around, a flower utters its name.[8] He laughs at the waterfall disheveled by the pine trees, then on the hilltop recognizes the goddess. Yves Bonnefoy (no doubt jokingly) found the "lièvre" saying its prayer in "Après le déluge" to be "mièvre" (affected); but isn't there something a bit cloying in this much-admired poem?

The next event in the poem brings to the surface a sublimated oedipal theme: the child begins to strip off the veils of the goddess, she who stands on the silver summit of the dawn. The immensity of the female figure versus the smallness of the child suggests an infantile memory. This transgressive act makes imagination run riot: "Dans l'allée, en agitant les bras. Par la plaine, où je l'ai dénoncée au coq. A la grand'ville elle fuyait parmi les clochers et les dômes, et courant comme un mendiant sur les quais de marbre, je la chassais" ("Down the path, waving my arms. Across the plain, where I denounced her to the cock. In the city she fled among the bell-towers and the domes, and running like a beggar across the marble quays, I chased her"). Here there is the same rhythmic phenomenon as at the start of the poem, sentences of increasing length as emotion builds to a climax:

> En haut de la route, près d'un bois de lauriers, je l'ai entourée avec ses voiles amassés, et j'ai senti un peu son immense corps.
>
> Where the road climbs, near a laurel wood, I embraced her bunched-up veils, and I felt gingerly her immense body.

Her veils are up around her waist (perhaps exposing her sex), he feels her divine flesh. . . . Emotion peaks after this profanatory deed and he passes out:

> L'aube et l'enfant tombèrent au bas du bois.
>   Au réveil il était midi.
>
> Dawn and the child fell at the edge of the wood.
>   When I woke up it was noon.

Rimbaud didn't need to learn the love of nature (animism if you will) from Hugo or Nerval. This was something he felt deeply, all his life, even years later in Africa. He hated many things about Africa, but the natural surroundings entranced him.

In "Aube" he takes the feelings that well up in that "heure indicible" and brings them, through personification and an intuitive rhythm, to a climax that ends abruptly, revealing, in that abruptness, its sexual nature. Think of the last line of "Conte": "La musique savante manque à notre désir."

MOST POEMS involve some kind of problem, crisis, conflict, or need. This may be the need to mourn a loved one; the need to speak out in delight; or the need to fill a psychic void. Or there may be the need to create a sense of inner order so that a nameless anxiety is dispelled. Ab-reaction—the impulsive movement away from a negative condition or feeling—is the process by which the problem is solved, the void filled, the anxiety dispelled. It involves the expression of and release from emotional tension through a symbolic activity that mediates the emotive charge and turns it back upon the subject, leading to resolution. In the physician's office abreaction may occur through the transference of the patient's needs onto the therapist, followed by a curative reabsorption of feelings back into the patient's psyche.

Emotion rises up in a psychic field between the subject and its object; but the object's presence is an illusion, just as the therapist is a delusive object, since the transference emotions are directed through him at others. What we desire, or, conversely, what we flee can never be wholly possessed: this is the root cause of affectivity. As Diotima describes it in Plato's *Symposium,* desire (i.e., emotion) is the ever unsatisfied child of Need. Emotion is a product of our contingency, the neediness of "the mewling and puking babe" brought brutally into the world. In this perspective, "Aube" becomes a compelling allegory for literary emotion. The poet seeks to possess the dawn, the gift of daylight that restores him to the world; but possession in its multifarious forms—seeing, stripping bare, describing, copulating—is evanescent, an illusion. He holds the dawn even as she sedates him. When he awakens, his brief emotive episode proves to have been only a dream.

Fantasy and Reality

"Vies I, II, III"; "H"

> A chaque être, plusieurs *autres* vies me semblaient dues.
> (To each being, several other lives seemed to me due.)
>
> —*Une Saison en enfer,* "Délires II"

A recurrent theme in *Illuminations* is the conflict between fantasy and reality. Rimbaud kept trying to come to terms with the reality principle, but his need for evasion was always stronger. He was always poised for flight—first to Paris, then to London and Brussels, then to Stuttgart or Java, and finally Africa. Jacques Rivière was the first critic to remark his profound need to be always somewhere else: "He shows a positive and even aggressive impossibility to 'exist in the world.'.... He suffocates, he squirms ceaselessly; always in vain. His continual flights are the fits and starts of that metaphysical intolerance . . . " (*Oeuvres,* 87). Rimbaud would start one project, then abandon it for another. When he was at home in Charleville (the place where he felt least at home), he would pick up ever-unfinished studies for his bachot (baccalaureate exam) or begin piano lessons with the upstairs neighbor. This need to be, in Baudelaire's formula, "Anywhere out of this world" appears in the poems called "Vies I, II, III" ("Lives I, II, III")."

"Vie I"

"Vie I" illustrates Rimbaud's recurrent dream of the Orient:

O les énormes avenues du pays saint, les terrasses du temple! Qu'a-t-on fait du brahmane qui m'expliqua les Proverbes? D'alors, de là-bas, je vois encore même les vieilles! Je me souviens des heures d'argent et de soleil vers les fleuves, la main de la campagne sur mon épaule, et de nos caresses debout dans les plaines poivrées.—Un envol de pigeons écarlates tonne autour de ma pensée.—Exilé ici j'ai eu une scène où jouer tous les chefs-d'oeuvre dramatiques de toutes les littératures. . . .

O the enormous avenues of the Holy Land, the terraces of the temple! what has become of the Brahmin who explained the Proverbs to me? From that time and place I can still see even the old women! I remember hours of sun and silver near the rivers, the countryside's hand on my shoulder, and our caresses as we stood on the spice-scented plains.—A flight of scarlet pigeons thunders about my thought.—Exiled here, I have had a stage on which to perform the dramatic masterpieces of all literatures. . . .

Sergio Sacchi says of this poem that " . . . everything in it suggests the slow progress of a daydream . . ." (Sacchi, 111) and Freud sees daydream or reverie as conscious fantasy; but, as we proceed, we will see that there are other types of fantasy in "Vies" as well. Fantasy is always linked with desire, and here we have two of Rimbaud's oldest desires, desire for a teacher and for a sexual partner. Sacchi comments that the rhythm "underlines the slow upward surge of memory . . . " (113). The poet remembers anecdotes and tales that show the Orient as a place where learning is held in high esteem and love is pantheistic, hence guilt-free. The silver of moonlight and the sunshine erase time as the landscape touches his shoulder. Sacchi reminds us that in "Sensation," written when he was sixteen, Rimbaud " . . . dreamed of losing himself in Nature—happy as with a woman . . . "(113). Yet a flight of pigeons interrupts the caress. This break suggests that guilt is present after all. The "ici / here and now" of his exile is not the Orient but the place where he is writing—the banal village of Roche (as becomes explicit in "Vie II"). The "scène," where, to escape from a tedious reality, he stages all the masterpieces of world literature, is in his mind. This image of theater insists on the urgency of his need to fantasize.

Sacchi comments on the passage that follows: "That feverish succession of narcissistic performances is in the first person . . . ("*Je* vous indiquerais . . . J'observe . . . Je vois / I will show you . . . I observe, I see"). Sacchi hears an echo of the same intonations found in "Nuit de l'enfer" in the *Saison:* "Je suis maître en fantasmagories... J'ai tous les talents... Je ferai de l'or, des remèdes / I'm a master in magic... I have every talent... I'll make gold, or medicines." Here the poet is a circus barker, trying to attract his audience (116).

But then poetic fantasy takes on the ambiance of a hellish dream. Rimbaud is performing for an audience that has lost interest. He is Mallarmé's "Pitre châtié / Punished Clown." Like Mallarmé's clown he removes his mask and speaks directly to the spectator of his inventions: he assures her he would have liked to show her "les richesses inouïes / unheard-of riches." She teases him, telling him the sequel. He is momentarily thrilled: "Je vois la suite! / I see the rest!" But his enthusiasm freezes. "Ma sagesse est aussi dédaignée que le chaos. Qu'est mon néant, auprès de la stupeur qui vous attend? / My insight is disdained like chaos. What is my nothingness compared to the stupor that awaits you?" The fantasy turns short, images flutter like pigeon wings. Rimbaud's "sagesse," acquired from the Brahman sage, is scorned by his imagined auditor. I read the last line as a veiled threat to her, like Ronsard's sonnet to the lady who had spurned him: "Quand vous serez bien vieille, au soir à la chandelle, / Assise auprès du feu, dévidant et filant / Direz chantez mes vers en vous émerveillant / Ronsard me célébrait du temps que j'étais belle" / "When you are very old, at evening by candlelight, / Seated by the fire, winding and spinning / You will sing my verse and marvel / Ronsard praised me when I was beautiful."

Rimbaud's "néant" is a failure of imagination; but it's still not as bad as the "stupeur" that awaits her, an ordinary person, doomed to the banality of bourgeois life.[1]

"Vie II"

"Vie II" involves self-definition and ego problems that Rimbaud remedies by fantasy:

> Je suis un inventeur bien autrement méritant que tous ceux qui m'ont précédé; un musicien même, qui ai trouvé quelque chose comme la clef de l'amour. A présent, gentilhomme d'une campagne aigre et sobre, j'essaye de m'émouvoir au souvenir de l'enfance mendiante, de l'apprentissage ou de l'arrivée en sabots, des polémiques, des cinq ou six veuvages, et quelques noces où ma forte tête m'empêcha de monter au diapason des camarades. Je ne regrette pas ma vieille part de gaîté divine: l'air sobre de

cette aigre campagne alimente fort activement mon atroce scepticisme. Mais comme ce scepticisme ne peut désormais être mis en oeuvre, et que d'ailleurs je suis dévoué à un trouble nouveau,—j'attends de devenir un très méchant fou.

I'm an inventor far more meritorious than all those who have preceded me; indeed a musician who has found something like the key of love. At present, squire of a harsh land with a sober sky, I try to feel emotion in remembering my mendicant childhood, my apprenticeship when I arrived wearing wooden shoes, my polemics, my five or six widowings, and a few binges when my strong head kept me from rising to the same pitch as my companions. I don't regret my old portion of divine gaiety: the sober air of this harsh countryside gives new vigor to my atrocious skepticism. But since this skepticism can no longer be put to use, and, since I am devoted to a new provocation,—I expect to become a very wicked fool.

The descriptive "une campagne aigre et sobre" suggests that Rimbaud wrote this at Roche before it was recopied by Germain Nouveau in 1874, while the pair were in London. He muses on his past, recalling the awkwardness of his arrival in Paris, figuratively "en sabots" (in wooden shoes). Rimbaud never forgot the humiliation of that first meeting, when he dined with Verlaine's wife and her parents. Next he recalls his quarrels and misunderstandings while consorting with Les Vilains Bonshommes; laments five or six unfortunate relationships; and brags that he could hold more alcohol than his comrades. If he does not feel guilty about his frequent bouts of drunkenness, why does he bother to say he doesn't regret "ma vieille part de gaîté divine"? Sacchi comments " . . . 'I don't regret' serves to exorcise a nostalgia or a regret only too real" (118). This place (and only his home town and the presence of his mother account for such bitterness) enhances "his atrocious skepticism." Then he predicts his eventual abandonment of poetry: "Mais comme ce scepticisme ne peut désormais être mis en oeuvre, et que d'ailleurs je suis dévoué à un trouble nouveau,—j'attends de devenir un très méchant fou."

The word "trouble" has a sexual connotation in French; this may be a reference to Germain Nouveau or simply some other commitment—plans to pass the bachot, to travel, and so on. Why has he given up his productive skepticism? I think that Rimbaud's biographers have not sufficiently assessed his guilt feelings, in regard to sexuality, intoxication, and the continuing practices of *Voyance*. His skepticism, his strongest defense against everything his mother stood for, is undermined by the necessity of playing at being "un gentilhomme." These were all things his mother knew about and disapproved of. Only guilt could produce such an extreme judgment: that he will soon become "a very wicked madman." It is said ironically, but there is a bitterness here that corresponds to the "campagne aigre au ciel sobre."

"Vie III"

"Vie III" recapitulates Rimbaud's fairy tale about his own life. He tells it ironically, with knowing exaggerations: The attic at Roche where he wrote *Une Saison en enfer* becomes "un grenier où je fus enfermé à douze ans / an attic where I was locked up at the age of twelve." The *bildungsroman* progression of *Une Saison* recalls Balzac's *Comédie humaine*. Antoine Adam notes that on a trip to Anvers he saw Rubens's portraits of his wives, Isabel and Helen. For the daydreamer, there is only a step more to actually meeting the wives of great painters. He allows the fantasy to expand to mythic proportions: "Dans une magnifique demeure cernée par l'Orient entier j'ai accompli mon immense oeuvre et passé mon illustre retraite / In a magnificent dwelling surrounded by the entire Orient I completed my prodigious work and spent my illustrious retirement."

EACH OF the three "Vies" begins expansively with a swell of poetic ego and then collapses as he reaches the end of his fantasy and returns to reality: "Mon devoir m'est remis. Il ne faut même plus songer à cela. Je suis réellement d'outre-tombe, et pas de commissions / My duty done, my brooding ended. I'm really out of this world and taking no further commissions."

These poems indicate that Rimbaud had painfully learned what Freud also discovered—that, although fantasy plays a major role in the etiology of neurosis, there is no sharp distinction between poetic genius and morbidity. In "Vie I" and "Vie III" in particular, there are grandiose fantasies that are suddenly terminated. "Vie I" ends with admission of his own nothingness. In II, although the fantasy is held in check, there is the threat of madness if he abandons his principal means of defense, fantasy production. In III he mimics the voice of Chateaubriand's *Les Mémoires d'outre-tombe*, and speaks to us from beyond the grave. All this shows that the abandonment of poetry was not an overnight process but a long and difficult trial, accomplished at the risk of his mental health. But he also realized that there were perhaps greater risks if he continued.

"*H*"

Another poem that should be considered in respect to the question of fantasy is "H," a poem generally agreed to refer to the act of masturbation. André Guyaux finds the key to "H" in the pairing *solitude-lassitude* which echoes the nominal pair *solitude-Habitude* in the satiric dizain on the Imperial Prince, "L'Enfant qui ramassa les balles." That poem (jokingly attributed to François Coppée) ends with the line: "Pauvre jeune homme, il a sans doute l'Habitude! / Poor young man, doubtless he has the Habit!" I think "H" deserves to be taken seriously, as an attempt to unwrap the complex imbrication of the mental and the physical involved in the act of onanism.

> Toutes les monstruosités violent les gestes atroces d'Hortense. Sa solitude est la mécanique érotique, sa lassitude, la dynamique amoureuse. Sous la surveillance d'une enfance elle a été, à des époques nombreuses, l'ardente hygiène des races. Sa porte est ouverte à la misère. Là, la moralité des êtres actuels se décorpore en sa passion ou en son action—O terrible frisson des amours novices, sur le sol sanglant et par l'hydrogène clarteux! trouvez Hortense.

> All forms of monstrosity violate the atrocious gestures of Hortense. Her solitude is erotic mechanics; her weariness, the dynamics of love. Under the supervision of childhood she has been, in numerous epochs, the ardent hygiene of races. Her door is open to poverty. There, the morality of actual beings is disembodied in her passion or her action.—O terrible thrill of novice loves on the bloody ground and in the milky hydrogen! find Hortense.

First, let me propose an answer to the enigma of "Hortense." Even if masturbation is habitual, it is accompanied by fantasy. Hortense Schneider (1838–1920), who starred in Offenbach's *La Belle Hélène* (1864), *La Grande Duchesse de Gérolstein* (1867), and *La Périchole* (1868), was also a famous courtesan. She had many lovers, including so many monarchs that she was nicknamed "le passage des princes." Zola took her as model for his heroine, Nana. Many thousands of Frenchmen (though not le Prince impérial, Napoléon IV, who was not even born when Schneider enchanted *le tout Paris*) must surely have fantasized the sensual soprano during their solitary pleasures.² The poem ends: "Trouvez Hortense!" But how do you find a fantasy? By *l'Habitude*. . . . But this identification, even if correct, stills leaves us with a dense and challenging poetic text. So let me push the analysis further.

If Hortense is a figure of fantasy, to whom atrocious gestures are attributed, she herself is violated by the monstrous fantasies of the onanist.³ The second line speaks of "her solitude . . . her weariness . . . "; this is a displacement of the possessive adjective from the actant to the acted upon. It is the onanist whose weary solitude has compelled him to have recourse to this parody of love's dynamic. Yet he will speak in her defense, for, from age to age, she has been "the ardent hygiene of races": masturbation is an outlet for urges that might otherwise lead to rape and violence.

"Her door is open to poverty." Those who cannot afford to buy sex have an alternative that is free to all. The next line is the most difficult in the poem: "There the morality of actual beings is disembodied in her passion or in her action." Once again, we find displacement of the possessive adjective: It is not *her* passion, *her* action, but *his;* and here the question of morality arises. We hear an echo of the confessional. It is Rimbaud who pronounces absolution upon the onanist: *Your action was merely a fantasy of an action, it was disembodied.* And the child leaves the confessional with an image of the bleeding earth, healed by the milky whiteness of semen. "Find Hortense"? A mere fantasy, Hortense has evaporated. Yet there is this *harmonie imitative:* The four expanding syllables of "trouvez Hortense," each longer in duration than the preceding, echo the "ithyphallique" of "Le Coeur du pitre" and are a sonorous embodiment of erection. If the title ("H") is the penis at rest, then the last two words ("trouvez Hortense") present it fully engorged.

10

Killing Me Softly[1]

"Conte"

> The price of Genet's fantastic power over reality is a parodistic simplification of reality.[2]

In its compactness and symmetry, "Conte" has a jewel-like quality; different facets sparkle plausibly in this polyvalent poem. "Conte" is often characterized as an enigma poem, that is, a puzzle to which there is a key. In her deconstructive reading of the poem, Barbara Johnson sees the enigma as the identity of the Prince. After showing that this identity is not a question of reference—the Prince is not Verlaine, Hamlet, Vathek, or Nero, etc.—she reaches the conclusion that everything in the puzzle refers back to itself: "Le Prince était le Génie. Le Génie était le Prince / The Prince was the Genie. The Genie was the Prince." Her reading sees the poem as a labyrinth of mirrors, where each entity reproduces itself in reverse: the assassinated wives reappear, the slaughtered pets revive, etc. The Prince and the Genie fuse into one.

There are innumerable readings of "Conte." Perhaps the two most diverse readings are those of André Guyaux, who finds the poem no more than a "brainwashing" for the typical Rimbaud devotee,[3] and that of James Lawler, who deciphers many levels of meaning in "Conte."

Lawler's study of Rimbaud is designed around the metaphor of theater, and his book reaches a high point in the lengthy and intricate analysis of this much discussed poem. I for one am convinced that, as Lawler argues, Baudelaire's "Une Mort héroïque" is the intertext that inspired Rimbaud's poem, even though "Conte" is lacking in several important features found in the prose poem by Baudelaire.[4] "Une Mort héroïque" presents us with a stage upon which Fanciulle, the supreme comic actor—specifically called "le génie"—reaches his sublime thespian peak and then, mortally wounded by a prank engineered by the Prince (a pageboy blows a whistle offstage), suddenly expires. There is no literal theater in "Conte," yet the poem might best be described by borrowing the title of Lawler's book, *Rimbaud's Theater of the Self.*

Baudelaire's explicit narrator is lacking in Rimbaud's poem. This narrator is the vehicle of emotion and, by his comments, adds a crucial dimension. So for instance the narrator writes, at the peak of Fancioulle's performance, "Ma plume tremble et des larmes d'une émotion toujours présente me montent aux yeux pendant que je cherche à vous décrire cette inoubliable soirée / My pen trembles and tears of an emotion still present flow from my eyes as I try to describe for you that unforgettable evening" (Baudelaire, *Oeuvres* I, 452).

IF ONE reflects on Baudelaire's story, it is apparent that both Fanciulle (Fanciullo, "boy" in Italian) and the Prince must have held a strong attraction for Rimbaud. The Prince was "Amoureux passionné des beaux-arts, excellent connaisseur d'ailleurs, il était vraiment insatiable de voluptés / A passionate lover of the arts, besides that a man of excellent taste, he was an insatiable lover of pleasure." Fanciulle is an artist "avec une joie qui l'empêche de voir la tombe / with a joy that prevents him from seeing the tomb."[5] He has the exuberance of a powerfully charismatic actor. Rimbaud's own narcissism is captured by the resemblance to himself of both the Genie and the Prince, and so, at the end of the poem, it is not surprising that he fuses them into one being:

> Un soir il [le Prince] galopait fièrement. Un Génie apparut, d'une beauté ineffable, inavouable même. De sa physionomie et son maintien ressortait la promesse d'un amour multiple et complexe! d'un bonheur indicible, insupportable même! Le Prince et le Génie s'anéantirent probablement dans la santé essentielle. Comment n'auraient-ils pas pu en mourir? Ensemble donc ils moururent.
>
> Mais ce Prince décéda, dans son palais à un âge ordinaire. Le prince était le Génie. Le Génie était le Prince.
>
> La musique savante manque à notre désir.

> One evening, when he was proudly galloping, a Genie appeared, of ineffable, inexpressible beauty. His appearance and his bearing gave promise of a multiple and complex love, of an unspeakable even unbearable

happiness. The Prince and the Genie destroyed each other, probably in the prime of life. How could they not have died of it? Thus together they died.

But this Prince passed away in his palace, at a normal age. The prince was the Genie. The Genie was the Prince.

The cunning music exhausts our desire.

One notable thing about "Conte" is the absence (or perhaps flatness) of emotion. This is not only because Rimbaud has removed the explicit narrator from Baudelaire's scenario, but because of the controlled, symmetrical way the poem is put together. The entire poem unfolds on the same affective level, as if something fundamental is being repressed. This is a feature Barbara Johnson has reproduced in her analysis. It too unfolds on the same level, in a progression of deconstructive clicks. Indeed, she uses "a parodistic simplification of reality" that coincides very closely with the logic of Rimbaud's text. It is a logic that reduces the poem to a *chassé-croisé*,[6] where terms change their meaning and position with the regularity of a dance. Johnson writes: "The Prince's quest, the constitutive *question* which determines the text is in reality an enigma, where the resolution (the Génie) is simply a different way of posing the question. . . . The 'word' [explanation] of the enigma, is nothing other, literally, than a word" (77).

Johnson seems to be saying that the poem involves the search for distraction; the answer to the Prince's search is his own simulacrum, in other words, himself. This puts us on the right track, for the poem is born out of primary narcissism. But there is something lacking in Johnson's analysis; a word is not enough. What can the Prince do, once he has discovered that he loves himself? The answer is closer to Genet than to Mallarmé, one of Johnson's points of reference.

As Rimbaud has told us in "H," masturbation is the refuge of the lonely, the bereft, the friendless. If such an individual has no one else to love, his residual narcissism allows him to love himself. This self-loving always has an accompanying fantasy.

The poem is about fantasies; and it starts with fantasies of destruction. In our discussion of "Après le déluge" the casual destructiveness of a child was seen as motive for the annihilation of the world. In "Conte," we see destrudo (the death wish) again, but this time as a feature of a despotic ruler, the Prince. Here it is not "the sudden death" (Fanciulle falls "roide mort") of Baudelaire's genius that Rimbaud's Prince wishes; rather, it is what is poetically known as "the little death." The progression of imperfects, ending with the past definite "Il voulut / he wished," suggests that we are dealing with a masturbation fantasy that has several near-climaxes but only attains *jouissance* (orgasm) at the end of the poem ("ils moururent / they died"). The word "death" has a long history of poetic equivalence with "sexual climax." This "conte" masquerades as a moral fable by La Fontaine or Voltaire; but it is really an erotic bedtime story. Habitually repeated on the threshold of sleep it becomes compacted, truncated, reduced to "the cunning music that exhausts our desire."

My reading of "H" in the preceding chapter halted briefly on the first line: "Toutes les monstruosités violent les gestes atroces d'Hortense. / All monstrosities violate the atrocious gestures of Hortense." There is general agreement among critics that "H" signifies l'Habitude which signifies masturbation; but where in "H" are the "monstruosités," where are the "gestes atroces," and what is the violation? I think here we are authorized to take a look backward, at "Le Coeur du pitre." That poem, also called "Le Coeur supplicié," is *all* emotion, from the first line to the last. Rimbaud was crushed by Izambard's cruel parody of his confessional work and never walked that path of vulnerability again. Enid Starkie was one of the first critics to remark the complete change in the young Rimbaud, when he returned home from *communard* Paris. She suggests that he was sexually attacked, and that along with the disgust and pain there was sexual pleasure. Later, his cohabitation with Verlaine involved roughhousing and downright violence.[7]

Destrudo

The destructiveness of "Conte" resembles that of "Après le déluge" in one curious respect. In "Après le déluge," the annihilated world is recreated. "Conte" has a symmetry that appears to be its central feature: the Prince, after remarking the beauty of his wives, destroys them; but they bounce back with magical resiliency. He admires, then kills his pet animals ("bêtes de luxe"); but they are resuscitated. Finally, he meets a Génie, perfect in every way; the Prince and this Génie, who promises "un bonheur indicible, insupportable même" ("an unspeakable, even unbearable happiness"), annihilate each other "probablement dans la santé essentielle" ("probably in the best of health" or "in the prime of life"), a euphemism for sexual intercourse. "Le Prince était le Génie. Le Génie était le Prince" ("The Prince was the Genie. The Genie was the Prince").

The last line is a chiasmus (a "crossing"), a device that provides a natural rhythmical ending: "La musique savante manque à notre désir." Chiasmus takes the form ABBA: A (Musique) B (Savante) B (Notre) A

(Désir)—the adjectives and nouns reverse position. Sexual energy is expended in orgasm, the story ends, as desire is momentarily exhausted. But soon desire returns, ready to repeat itself. And nobody has died; these deaths are only the effacement of fantasies, not the quietus of substantive beings—or even characters. Yet Rimbaud has given his answer to the enigma of love. There are those who fall in love with their own self-image: the word of the enigma is "Narcissus." This impels us to return to another feature of the poem singled out by Guyaux, the "casade of negative adjectives" in the paragraph where the Genie meets the Prince: "inéffable, inavouable même . . . un bonheur indicible, insupportable même! / ineffable, even unmentionable . . . an unspeakable happiness, unbearable even!" This is not "brainwashing" but, rather, the description of a happiness that is no happiness, a love that is no love because it is directed at a non-object, oneself.

THERE IS another important issue that remains to be dealt with—the issue of violence. In his essay "Persons in Pieces," Leo Bersani writes of Genet's *Pompes Funèbres:* "The brutality of Genet's sexual fantasies suggests the masturbator's murderous intolerance of whatever spoils his exciting sexual inventions. The onanist is a rigorous novelistic plotter. He crudely dramatizes the self-projectiveness of all literary invention, and primitively and melodramatically, he reveals the evil of love and literature as a desire to coerce the world into being an exciting replica of the self" (288).

The "rigorous" plot is much more obvious in Rimbaud's poem of twenty-nine lines than in Genet's novel. This "symmetry," as I have called it, is one of the poem's main features, a feature that points to its character as a sexual fantasy. The "evil of love and literature" is overt in Genet's novel; in Rimbaud's "Conte," the artificiality of the fable negates the attribution of evil. The only immorality we might attribute to it is the egoism of the Prince, his relentless focus on his own pleasure. But isn't this exactly the mindset of the onanist?

Sartre called his book on the author of *Pompes Funèbres* "Saint Genet"; and this was not only to echo the *Saint Genest* of Rotrou. In his systematic reversal of values, Genet is a saint of evil, a being who, like the Prince of "Conte," kills before he can love. Lawler's reading of "Conte" as a parable of mystical love—i.e., a reversal of Genet's reversal—is a daring interpretation of this polyvalent text. Certainly "Conte" is not, as Guyaux contends, an exercise in brainwashing; but the love at issue here is lacking in the power that we attribute to the great mystical poets, such as Hafiz or John of the Cross, to follow Lawler's interpretation.

WHY CALL the poem a masturbation fantasy instead of a fantasy *tout court*? Why *this* wish? Perhaps there is ecstasy in destruction, rejuvenation in cruelty, especially when these are figments of imagination. Psychoanalyst Daniel Lagache notes that vitality, sexuality, and love are all linked with aggression, in the "looking-glass self" of the young child.[8] I concur with this comment from Lawler: "ecstacy may perhaps be found in destruction, youthful vigor in cruelty . . . " (149).

Graham Robb's biography, the most recent, the most outspoken in its revelation of Rimbaud's flaunting, outrageous, and often obscene behavior from 1871 when he first took up with Verlaine, until the summer of 1873, focuses on the dark side of Rimbaud's character.[9] As Lawler suggests, the adolescent Rimbaud found pleasure in destruction. Especially when destruction was merely fantasized.

11
"Nocturne vulgaire" and the Paranoid Position

This poem, probably written under the influence of hashish, combines four visions: the poet is not only in a phantasmagoric theater where sets rise, collapse, and combine: "Un souffle ouvre des brèches opéradiques dans les cloisons, / —brouille le pivotement des toits rongés,—disperse les limites des foyers" / "A breath opens operatic fissures in the walls,—blurs the pivoting of the rotting ceilings,—dispels the limits of the hearths"; but he is also staring into the flames of a fire: "Un vert et un bleu très foncés envahissent l'image / A very deep green and blue invade the image [second vision]." Simultaneously, he seems to be in a dream state, witnessing his own funeral: "Corbillard de mon sommeil, isolé, maison de berger de ma niaiserie, le véhicule vire sur le gazon de la grande route effacée; et dans un défaut en haut de la glace de droite tournoient les blêmes figures lunaires, feuilles, seins / Hearse of my hidden slumber, shepherd's hut of my silliness, the vehicle swerves on the grass of the obliterated highway [third vision]; and in a blemish at the top of the right hand window [fourth vision] swirl pale lunar figures, leaves, breasts." And finally, he is Jack of the Beanstalk, who climbs through the jagged holes in the ceilings ("toits rongés") and then down again: "Le long de la vigne, m'étant appuyé du pied à une gargouille [the giant]—je suis descendu dans ce carrosse . . . / Down the length of the vine, leaning with one foot against the gargoyle, I came down into this coach. . . . "

What psychoanalytic paradigm can account for this unity in difference? Stephen Mitchell and Margaret Black make this comparison that provides an appropriate template for the poem:

> For Freud the psyche is shaped through the oedipal conflict into stable and coherent structures, with hidden recesses and illicit designs. In an increasingly dramatic although unannounced fashion, Klein substituted for Freud's vision a portrayal of mind as a continually shifting, kaleidoscopic stream of primitive, phantasmagoric images, fantasies, and terrors. For Klein, the psyche, not just of the small child but of the adult as well, remains always unstable, fluid, constantly fending off psychotic anxieties. For Freud, each of us struggles with bestial wishes, fears of retribution, and guilt. For Klein, each of us struggles with the deep terrors of annihilation (paranoid anxiety) and utter abandonment (depressive anxiety).[1]

A Kleinian reading of this poem seems feasible when we realize that drugs—and this is a hashish trance—can produce transient psychotic states. The breast imagery is also Kleinian: "—je suis descendu dans ce carrosse dont l'époque est assez indiquée par les glaces convexes, les panneaux bombés et les sophas contournés— / I landed in this coach whose period is apparent in the convex windows, the swelling panels and the rounded sofas. . . . " Later in the same paragraph, the poet explicitly uses the word "breasts." The breast is the child's first object, and he expends his early instinctual emotions upon it (greed, anxiety, etc.).[2] The ambivalence of infantile desire, which sees the breast as generous and refusing, good and bad, is present throughout the poem in various couplings: "vert et bleu / green and blue," "les Sodomes, et les Solymes / Sodoms and Solesmses," "les bêtes féroces et les armées / ferocious beasts and armies." His appetites can be gauged by the penultimate verset—reminiscent of "Le Bateau ivre":

> —Et nous envoyer, fouettés à travers les eaux clapotantes et les boissons répandues, rouler sur l'aboi des dogues . . .

> —And send us, whipped over the splashing waves and spilled drinks, to roll over the barking of the bulldogs . . .

The poem ends as it begins, with a breath, an act akin to the suckling of an infant: "—Un souffle disperse les limites du foyer / —A breath dispels the limits of the hearth." The final line recalls other such downbeats of the conductor's bow, as in "Conte," where "La musique savante manque à notre désir."

One question about "Nocturne vulgaire" that has not been adequately addressed concerns the second word of the oxymoronic title. Suzanne Bernard attributes it to the fact that this highly musical "Nocturne" is the product of a hashish dream. I think it is not the "vulgarity" of hashish, a bizarre attribution, but rather the fact that it is outside a theater or concert hall, in the poet's room, either a day-by-day rental or a hotel room in London or Paris. How many great poems have been written in such vulgar surroundings?

Bernard emphasizes the poem's musicality, giving this quote from Rivière: "He [Rimbaud] knows the correct vibrato of every vowel; he takes each as a musical note and writes its harmonics . . . " (*Oeuvres,* 563, n8).

The poem's overture is announced by the rhythmic development of the first lines, where primary accents on four verbs ("ouvre," "brouille," "disperse," "éclipse") mark a complex prosodic unit. The urgent rhythm prepares us for "Jack's" leap to the beanstalk, his bold step on the monster's head, then his mysterious insertion into the funeral procession of his own sleep: "Corbillard de mon sommeil. . . . " This prepares his onirique regression into a mysterious world inhabited by "blêmes figures lunaires, feuilles, seins."

Is the pale moonlike figure the naked father imago, covered by a figleaf? Are the breasts those of Mme Cloutier, his wet nurse, those of his mother, or of " . . . la fille aux tétons énormes / the girl with enormous tits" ("Au Cabaret-Vert")? Maybe he's seen a music hall chorus line? Maybe even the breasts of "Hortense" come to haunt his dreams. The entire section, from "Corbillard" to "seins" has a broken rhythm, produced by secondary or even tertiary relays within the passage. So "*Corbillard* de *mon* som*meil*" forms the first rhythmic unit; then "*isolé*" which picks up the rhyme, relays us into "maison de berger de ma niaiserie. . . ." The silliness may be caused by hashish, brought to an abrupt halt by what he sees in the tarnished mirror ("un défaut en haut de la glace de droite"): the father and mother imago. We recall that Klein considers "the earliest anxiety situation of all to be . . . the struggle with the father's penis in the mother."[3]

There are serious questions about when and how the hallucination becomes a poem. How do infantile drives take on form and integrate with adult perceptions? Here I want to quote from Joseph Pineau's book on

French speech rhythms: "Thus, only rhythm, through whatever form it takes and whatever its amplitude, makes the passage of time bearable for humankind."[4] Time is indeed an issue in "Nocturne vulgaire." The repetition of "Un souffle" at beginning and end implies that the poem is instantaneous, outside of all temporality. (This use of repetition brings to mind a modern work: Cocteau's film, *Le Sang d'un poète / Blood of a Poet* [1932], which begins and ends with the same crumbling smoke stack.)

Observe the notational style at several points—in the lines beginning "Corbillard de mon sommeil ... ," where in each prosodic unit the verb is deferred; also in "Dételage aux environs d'une tache de gravier / Unharnessing near a pile of gravel"; here, time is slowed if not suspended. The parenthetical question ("Postillon et bêtes de songe reprendront-ils sous les plus suffocantes futaies, pour m'enfoncer jusqu'aux yeux dans la source de soie? / Will the postilion and dream animals return in the most stifling furrows, to submerge me to eye level in the silken wellspring?") is the crux of the poem, the point at which infantile anxiety—paranoia—reaches its peak: the postilion/father, aided by shadowy dream animals, holds the child's head under water and he almost drowns. The parentheses work in two contradictory ways: they both emphasize the event and put it out of play. The dreamer flees, dogs barking at his heels. . . .

The rhythm is managed in such a way as to produce a cumulative effect: dazzlement, self-revelation, and self-witholding. Momentarily we share the dream, we ourselves become phantoms of the opera; we share the poet's impulses which become our own, and in that brief fusion, are taken deeper into ourselves than we have ever been before. Amid these terrors we confront love and destructiveness, till we slide down the beanstalk and leave horror behind; but not so fast—"Un souffle disperse les limites du foyer." The fireplace, the room, the shelter that we call home—all vanish in a breath as quickly as they had come. The aftereffects of paranoia continue while we sleep, submerged to our eyelids in "la source de soie / the silken spring," until we have metabolized the drug out of our system.

V

"O fecundity of the mind and immensity of the universe!"

12

"Génie"

Advent of the Ego-Ideal

Bonnefoy writes: "'Génie' is an act of stunning intuition, that instant of shadowless intuition when a thought is realized" (144). What thought is realized here, what intuition given material form?

A widely accepted view takes the poem to advance a new form of Love, as propounded by the social romanticism associated with Michelet and Quinet.[1] In his book *Le Génie des Religions* (1842), Edgar Quinet interrogates the human spirit, finding within it a searching, unquiet passion out of which arise the varied forms of the divine. These gods (of Judaism, Christianity, Islam, etc.), gods made in the image and likeness of man, in turn produce the political institutions that characterize each civilization. Rimbaud was attracted by the cohesiveness of Quinet's approach, this unification of all human culture into a single evolving syntagma. From that point it took only an intuitive leap of poetic insight to transform this impersonal impulse, working its way up and through the amalgam of cultures, into a single individual, to personify the *élan vital*, giving it the shape and characteristics of a godlike being.

The process that Rimbaud follows in poetizing Quinet's concept is similar to that which, according to Freud, the human individual follows in creating his or her "ego-ideal." This is the psychic paradigm that we conceive as the object of our dreams and desires, the inner being whose authority we follow, whom we imitate and, as we become adults, learn to serve, to obey, to respect, and to love. It is indeed our genie, our daemon; an "other" that is also our self. This, according to Freud, is where our highest cultural values come into play:

> It is easy to show that the ego ideal answers to everything that is expected of the higher nature of man. As a substitute for a longing for the father, it contains the germ from which all religions have evolved. The self-judgment which declares that the ego falls short of its ideal produces the religious sense of humility to which the believer appeals in his longing. As a child grows up, the role of the father is carried on by teachers and others in authority; their injunctions and prohibitions remain powerful in the ego ideal. . . . Social feelings rest on identifications with other people, on the basis of having the same ego ideal.[2]

The ego-ideal (which Freud sees as part of the super-ego[3]) is the product of the individual's personal history, yet also embodies broader cultural values. Freud writes in another context:

> Thus a child's super-ego is in fact constructed on the model not of its parents but of its parents' super-ego; the contents which fill it are the same and it becomes the vehicle of tradition and of all the time-resisting judgments of value which have propagated themselves in this manner from generation to generation.[4]

The ego-ideal, then, is the repository of history where traditions breed and reform, giving each community the guidance it needs to survive. It serves each individual to the degree that he or she has had the good fortune to live by the "sacred" values (that which is set apart and worshiped) of a time and place. In the case of Rimbaud, given the rarity of contact with his father and the bigotry of his mother, we must view the formation of his ego-ideal (as exemplified in this poem) as a miracle of inner fortitude, intelligence, and perseverance. To follow our Génie is to live truthfully; this is the ideal to which Rimbaud aspired from the age of seven, when he had to separate himself from the moral dishonesty of his mother; when he began to discover the reality of who and what he was, distinct from the accretions of time, place, and convention, yet conditioned by them.

> Il est l'affection et le présent puisqu'il a fait la maison ouverte à l'hiver écumeux et à la rumeur de l'été, lui qui a purifié les boissons et les aliments, lui qui est le charme des lieux fuyants et le délice surhumain des

stations. Il est l'affection et l'avenir, la force et l'amour que nous, debout dans les rages et les ennuis, nous voyons passer dans le ciel de tempête et les drapeaux d'extase.

He is affection and the present since he has thrown open the house to the frothy winter and to the sounds of summer, he who has purified drinks and food, he who is the charm of fleeting places and the superhuman delight of rest areas. He is affection and the future, the force and love that we, standing in rages and boredoms, see passing in the tempestuous sky and the flags of ecstasy.

The poem begins with the triple repetition "Il est . . . / He is . . . ", enunciating the Génie's major qualities: "Il est l'affection et le présent . . ."; "Il est l'affection et l'avenir . . . "; "Il est l'amour. . . . "

This is a syllogism: if he is affection and the present, but also affection and the future, thus, since he commands all time, he personifies love. Just as Jesus made wine from water and multiplied loaves and fishes, so the Génie has purified all drinks and foodstuffs, because he is the charm of passing sights and the delight of stations.

Repetition with variations is the rhetorical form of litany as are the repeated ejaculations—note the frequency of exclamation marks. Yet the poem does not have the deadening regularity of litany, making it, as Lawler suggests, more in keeping with the form of an inspired sermon. As the god figure develops, we see that Rimbaud has drawn on his experience of Christianity; yet nowhere in his work does he express devotion to the Christ persona. In fact, he writes in "Les Premières Communions": "Christ! ô Christ, éternel voleur des énergies . . . / Christ! O Christ, eternal thief of energies. . . . " This is not any recognizable god; and, as the poem progresses, we understand why certain critics (René Char and Wallace Fowlie, to name only two) have identified the god with the poet himself. No doubt because the god is the *projection* of the poet, the ideal being he might wish to become. Here an important distinction must be made, one that psychoanalyst Daniel Lagache insists upon in his neo-Freudian account of the ego:

> Let us return to the problem of the internal structure of the ego [le moi]. The issues considered earlier led us to introduce here the distinction between a constituted ego and a constituting ego. The constituted ego is an agent of defensive behaviors, automatic and unconscious, motivated by the id and the super-ego, and driven by the urgency to reduce

unpleasant affects and painful tensions. The self-constituting ego is differentiated from this by its resistance to tensions and to repetition; it aspires to the realization of the possibilities of the subject; it engages the highest forms of conscious activity, of attention and reflection, of judgment and will; it bases its action on the categories of objective rational thought, on the input of the psychoanalyst; in the final analysis, its external resources allow it to affirm its autonomy in relation to its constituted ego, proceeding then to a restructuring of the psychological field, in an action both destructive and constructive.[5]

Rimbaud's Génie, his ego-ideal, was not born passively, out of fear and a consequent defensiveness; it was born out of the child's defiance, the adolescent's searching intelligence. It was born out of love:

> Il est l'amour, mesure parfaite et réinventée, raison merveilleuse et imprévue, et l'éternité: machine aimée des qualités fatales. Nous avons tous eu l'épouvante de sa concession et de la nôtre: ô jouissance de notre santé, élan de nos facultés, affection égoïste et passion pour lui, lui qui nous aime pour sa vie infinie . . .

> He is love, measure perfect and reinvented, reason marvelous and unforeseen, and eternity; adored machine of fatal qualities. We have all known the terror of his concession and of our own: O rapture of our health, transport of our powers, egoistical affection and passion for him, for him who loves us out of his infinite life . . .

The comparison with a "machine" might surprise, but in the nineteenth century there was a Romantic infatuation with the power and dependability of machines; while behind this contemporary metaphor (e.g., the locomotive and other industrial machines) lies the vast machinery of heaven, the procession of the stars and planets, as charted by the ancient Greeks. Here, the reference points to the overwhelming attraction of the Génie. He erases all the vicissitudes of love; in his presence we realize our potential for health and well-being. The phrase "affection égoïste" refers back to the origin of the ego-ideal in childish narcissism, a state left behind as we reach adulthood and learn to love and respect a being both ontologically real—a composite of our life experience—and imaginary, created out of all we have seen as admirable, a being who comes to embody all that is noble in us. This is, implicitly, a justification for religious faith in an idealized being, whose power is multiplied many times over by the numbers of people who share commitment to him. It is a fundamental human process that shows us how men may create gods; but also, how they may come to recognize their God.

> Et nous nous le rappelons et il voyage.... Et si l'Adoration s'en va, sonne, sa promesse sonne: "Arrière ces superstitions, ces anciens corps, ces ménages et ces âges. C'est cette époque-ci qui a sombré!"
>
> Il ne s'en ira pas, il ne redescendra pas d'un ciel, il n'accomplira pas la rédemption des colères de femmes et des gaïtés des hommes et de tout ce péché: car c'est fait, lui étant, et étant aimé.
>
> O ses souffles, ses têtes, ses courses; la térrible célérité de la perfection des formes et de l'action.
>
> O fécondité de l'esprit et immensité de l'univers!

> And we recall him and he travels.... And if Adoration vanishes, resounds, resounds his promise: "Away with these superstitions, these wasting bodies, these households and these ages. It is this very age that has foundered!"
>
> He will not leave us, he will not come down from heaven, he will not redeem the anger of women or the revels of men or of all this sin: for it is accomplished, he being and being loved.
>
> O his breaths, his expressions, his journeys: the terrible swiftness of the perfection of forms and of action!
>
> O fecundity of the mind and immensity of the universe!

It is apparent that Rimbaud's Génie is both a personal and a collective creation. "Il voyage...." He is simultaneously everywhere in the world; "sa promesse sonne...." His revelation is heard throughout the world. Here, Rimbaud is a prophet speaking of the fidelity of this god figure who acquires greater reality as the poem progresses. This is the same process by which Mohammed gave substance to Allah and the Evangelists to Jesus, their Lord and Teacher. Here the poem demonstrates the power of language, its ability to give life to its deepest, most strongly felt visions.

The Génie is a figure of great ethical stature: "Arrière ... Away with these superstitions, 'ces anciens corps' / these 'uncorrupted remains' of saints or other idols; away with 'ces ménages' / couples and their 'family values' ... " We remember that Jesus said: "I bring not peace but a sword...." And further, we should not be surprised by the fact that the Génie shares Rimbaud's personal values, since he is Rimbaud's ego-ideal. He is the idealized figure that Rimbaud would follow into the fiery furnace; he exists in the here and now, Rimbaud recognizes him in the passions of his own soul; yet he is as immense as the universe. In this way, he is both immanent and transcendent. Throughout history, many individuals have created cults, imagined deities, propounded ethical standards; usually we call them fanatics, zealots, madmen. Yet Rimbaud's poem avoids excess, it is immanent to the poet and makes no demands; the Génie bestows his gift and passes on.

There is another important feature of "Génie" that reminds us it is a poem and not a revelation; it is the way the poem's rhythm builds to an ecstatic climax, taking the speaker outside of himself, thereby giving the ego-ideal its own separate "existence," while retaining Rimbaud's signature. It is, finally, the poem's ascencional rhythm that makes us participants not in the creation of a god but in a celebration of reverence for human possibilities. Who would not follow such a hymnist, such a master?

Consider the second paragraph, quoted earlier: "Il est l'amour, mesure parfaite et réinventée. . . . " The "il est" litany ends in a cascade of nouns and nominal phrases, piling one upon the other, concluding with the enigmatic "machine aimée des qualités fatales." We saw this as the Grecian vision of the heavens; but Rimbaud's Génie is also part of the inexorable Machine of modernity, driven by Reason. We have been terrified by all this offers to us and all it requires:

> Nous avons tous eu l'épouvante de sa concession et de la nôtre: ô jouissance de notre santé, élan de nos facultés, affection égoïste et passion pour lui, lui qui nous aime pour sa vie infinie. . . .
>
> We have all felt the terror of his concession and our own: O rapture of our health, transport of our faculties, egoist affection and passion for him, he who loves us for his infinite life. . . .

Here the "ô" is followed by the powerful word "jouissance" with its three syllables and the lingering triphthong "oui"—the very word speaks affirmation. In this passage he voices a fundamental reciprocity between the supreme being and ourselves. We create our ego-ideal, but it serves us by expanding our own potentiality.

THE GÉNIE is for all peoples, not to adore but to give to each according to his need; his promise echoes the messianism of Proudhon and Marx. But after promise, condemnation. Each short decree is bitten off, show-

Chapter 12. "Génie": Advent of the Ego-Ideal

ing what he will *not* do; and the verset ends with a solemn judgment, the repeated participle "étant / being" building upon the universality of his existence and his being loved.

Then the litany of Os breaks forth, now song more than chant:

> O ses souffles, ses têtes, ses courses; la térrible célérité de la perfection des formes et de l'action!
> O fécondité de l'esprit et immensité de l'univers!

> O his breaths, his expressions, his journeys; the terrible speed of the perfection of forms and action!
> O fecundity of the spirit and immensity of the universe!

The poem builds upon a series of nominal affirmations, where ellipsis shows that the reader is taken into the poet's confidence, since he or she must supply the missing verbs: "Son corps! Le dégagement rêvé, le brisement de la grâce croisée de violence nouvelle!" ("His body! The dreamed disengagement, the breaking of grace inbred with new violence!")

"Dégagement" is the balletic move where one foot glides as weight is shifted from the opposite leg; but this contained motion also suggests the radical perspectival change associated with Heidegger, where entities are irradiated by the power of a new consciousness:

> Sa vue, sa vue! . . .[6]
> Son jour . . .
> Son pas! les migrations plus énormes que les anciennes invasions!

> His vision, his vision! . . .
> His day . . .
> His step! migrations more enormous than the ancient invasions!

This is an apparent borrowing from Quinet, who describes how migrating tribes and nations disseminate their gods. We are lifted to a state of lyrical enthusiasm by the serial declaratives, as the poet calls on our intuition to give form and substance to the god seen through the veil of his rapid phrases.

The last paragraph reprises earlier nouns (ses souffles, son corps) and forces into one complex sentence a last imperative that is also an appeal: "Sachons . . . le héler et le voir, et le renvoyer . . . et suivre ses vues, ses souffles, son corps, son jour / May we know . . . to hail and see him, and to send him on his way ... and to follow his visions, his breaths, his body, his day."

Even though "Génie" involves a rejection of Christ ("il ne s'en ira pas, il ne redescendra pas d'un ciel"), it is clear that Rimbaud has a profound, lived understanding of what an authentic religious commitment should be. The god-figure must be greeted (le héler), he must be seen and imitated (suivre ses vues), but he is not the exclusive property of any church: we must always send him on his way. In loving God we possess the whole world ("de cap en cap, du pôle tumultueux au château, de la foule à la plage ... / from cape to cape, from the tumultuous pole to the castle, from the crowd to the beach ... "), we take our health from him, our perspective must be as broad as his (ses vues), and he gives us life itself (son jour).

By the power of poetic projection, Rimbaud manifests the god within. His own ego-ideal, formed out of residual religious experiences, expanded by his own moral and spiritual impulses, becomes a numinous figure who shows him the path he must follow in life. To us also the *Génie* stands as a being who calls to the ego-ideal in each of us, who gives us courage to resist "les malheurs nouveaux / new misfortunes" and, while the day lasts, shows us the incarnational power of language. Paul Claudel has first and best expressed our debt to Rimbaud: "Formes, pensée et principes, je lui dois tout et je me sens avec lui les liens qui peuvent vous rattacher à un ascendant spirituel / Forms, thought and principles, I owe him everything and I feel between us such ties as bind you to a spiritual ancestor."[7]

13

Narcissistic Gain in "Solde"

> Ultimately for a poet the fence is so high the top is invisible, but it is what we are designed to reach for.
>
> —Jim Harrison[1]

This poem is based on anaphora, the repetition of the same initial phrase ("A vendre") to produce a cumulative effect:

> A vendre ce que les Juifs n'ont pas vendu, ce que noblesse ni crime n'ont goûté, ce qu'ignorent l'amour maudit et la probité infernale des masses: ce que le temps ni la science n'ont pas à reconnaître . . .

> For sale what the Jews haven't sold, what neither nobility nor crime has tasted, what forbidden love and the hellish honesty of the masses ignore: what neither time nor science is obliged to recognize . . .

"Solde" can considered as adjunct to "Génie." It shows the corrupted world into which the Génie comes and which he must redeem by his constantly reinvented love. It is a world viewed depressively, a commercialized world where everything is for sale. The prejudice of "A vendre ce que les Juifs n'ont pas vendu" is a cliché or an automatism. There is no other trace of anti-Semitism in Rimbaud. "Solde" begins with Rimbaud's auction of all he most values, as if to say, *Here it is, I'm giving it away!* This tone of feigned self-liquidation explains why the poem is sometimes seen in tandem with "la lettre du voyant," where he first initiates themes that reappear in "Solde." So, for example, "Toutes les formes d'amour /

All forms of love" might be considered to appear in the lettre du voyant as "l'amour maudit / forbidden love"; "Il est chargé de l'humanité / he is in command of humanity" might appear as "l'éveil fraternel de toutes les énergies chorales et orchestrales et leurs applications instantanées / the fraternal awakening of all choral and orchestral energies"; "le temps d'un langage universel viendra / the time of a universal language will come" as "Les trouvailles et les termes non soupçonnés / the unforeseen discoveries and terminology. . . ." This comparison appears plausible if we consider that Rimbaud's career is just beginning in the letter to Izambard and Demeny in May 1871 (la lettre du voyant) but is winding down at the time of "Solde" (precise date unknown). He would then be writing "Solde" out of caustic irony and embitterment. The gratification that accompanies this poetic exercise is not achieved through attainment of an object but is based on the pride Rimbaud takes in being able to say: *I search the ineffable: who is rich enough to buy my talent?*

EARLIER POEMS such as "Qu'est-ce pour nous, mon coeur . . . " are recalled by the second paragraph:

> Les Voix reconstitués; l'éveil fraternel de toutes les énergies chorales et orchestrales et leurs applications instantanées; l'occasion, unique, de dégager nos sens!

> Reconstituted Voices: the brotherly awakening of all choral and orchestral energies and their instantaneous applications; the unique chance to disengage our senses!

The last line echoes the "dégagement rêvé . . . " of "Génie": disengagement of our senses from trivial things, from mere appearances. Here we find again the Heideggerean vision of "entities" that I have associated with *Voyance* and Rimbaud's radical poetics. But there is this important difference between the two: Heidegger says that "the poet bids things to come" and while there is "pain" at the threshold where language arises, it is not comparable to the violence and the urgency of *Voyance*.[2] Rimbaud *looks toward Heidegger,* he anticipates the path and senses the dwelling place that Heidegger will find; he learns the mirror-play of earth and sky, but far too soon; and there is no one to guide him. His suffering is greater; and his solitude, starting in his early twenties, is like that of the ex-convicts he admired as a small boy, a life sentence.[3]

In the phenomenological reach of Rimbaud's visionary poetics, things are seen with enhanced luster. There is a desperate quality in his grasping for the ineffable and this ratchets up their cost:

> Elan insensé et infini aux splendeurs invisibles, aux délices insensibles, et ses secrets affolants pour chaque vice—et sa gaîté effrayante pour la foule—

> Senseless and infinite leap toward invisible splendors, to delights beyond sense, and their maddening secrets for each vice—and its terrifying gaiety for the crowd—

The poet takes pride in his vision, a gift that can't be sold or given away. Having disengaged from material things, his pride (one of the few things he has left) leads to a deepened sense of self-value; pride helps him to overcome obstacles and frustrations.[4] And again there is "narcissistic gain" (258) in the delight of words that surpass thought and breath, in the possessing of "splendeurs invisibles" within the very core of self; and there are "délices insensibles / imperceptible delights," hardly felt yet present in the functioning of mind and body, while the pen flies across the page. All this occurs in spite of the shallow commercialism around him. How hard it was to maintain self-esteem, to continue writing in the face of indifference and ostracism, without an audience, without guaranteed publication!

"Secondary gain" is sometimes seen in conjunction with illness or neurosis: it may consist of attracting attention, being loved or, as psychoanalyst Otto Fenichel puts it, "a right to privileges; these privileges may consist of material gains or of more subtle mental gains."[5] The term is expandable, and one can see the struggles of many literary figures, unsuccessful in their own times, as an effort to attain secondary gain. But Fenichel avers that the search for satisfaction by a display of temper (as in this poem) is not a mature response, i.e., not "in accordance with the reality principle" (453). No doubt Rimbaud's long and painful maturation was one of the factors that caused him to abandon poetry.

HERE, Rimbaud's pride becomes aggressive. He throws his jewels before swine: "Solde de diamants sans contrôle! / Diamonds for sale for the asking!" In offering his own riches, he is also passing judgment on the commercialism of his time. In nineteenth-century France, you can have it all! Learn how to make your Bodies beautiful, find the partner of your dreams: "A vendre les Corps sans prix, hors de toute race, de tout monde, de tout sexe, de toute descendance! / For sale priceless Bodies, beyond any race, any society, any sex, or any ethnicity!"

Move into your dream house:

> A vendre les habitations et les migrations, sports, féeries et comforts parfaits, et le bruit, le mouvement et l'avenir qu'ils font!
>
> A vendre les applications de calcul et les sauts d'harmonie inouïs. Les trouvailles et les termes non soupçonnées, possession immédiate.
>
> For sale habitations and migrations, sports, fairylands and perfect comforts, and the sounds, the movement and the future they contain!
>
> For sale applied arithmetic and the shifts of unheard harmonies. Discoveries and terms never suspected, immediate possession.

Buy now, pay later—it's the refrain that rhymes our days and nights; but, to hear this poem and to judge the spurious luxury it proposes, we have to understand the misery in which Rimbaud lived most of his life, the lack of comfort and often of necessities.

"Vagabonds" describes his life in common with Verlaine, often wretched, lacking in most necessities: "Pitoyable frère! Que d'atroces veillées je lui dus! 'Je ne me saisissais pas fervemment de cette entreprise. Je m'étais joué de son infirmité . . . ' / Pitiful brother! How many atrocious vigils he cost me! 'I wasn't fervently committed to this enterprise. I exploited his weakness. . . . '"

It was so easy to push Verlaine's buttons, to turn him from a sensible comrade into a raving hysteric.[6] A poor sort of life for a nineteen-year-old boy who wanted friendship, nurture, love. Rimbaud's life as a poet was marginal. The story of his travels back and forth between Charleville, Paris, and Belgium, his scandalous behavior and the humiliation it brought on him, this was only part of his life during those years. He was unemployed, scraping by tutoring French in London, often hungry, hung-over, consumed by anxiety and doubt. During his two years on and off with Verlaine, they lived in a love-hate relationship aggravated by absinthe and hashish. He never speaks of new clothes and rejects "féeries et comforts parfaits."[7] Public baths were available but are never mentioned; probably the vagabonds could only rarely afford them. His will never be "le Corps sans prix / the priceless Body."

"Vagabonds" ends:

J'avais en effet, en toute sincérité d'esprit, pris l'engagement de le rendre à son état primitif de fils du soleil,—et nous errions, nourris du vin des cavernes et du biscuit de la route, moi pressé de trouver le lieu et la formule.

I had in all sincerity, pledged to restore him to his primal state as a child of the sun,—and we wandered, nourished by the wine of caverns and wayside biscuits, I hard pressed to find the place and the formula.

Bonnefoy sees the phrase "fils du soleil" as a sign of Rimbaud's Gnosticism, his harking back (like Nietzsche) to ancient occult sources; and perhaps indeed this is an example of the Nietzschean will-to-power, a self-surpassing that Rimbaud tried to impose upon his friend. Suzanne Bernard puts it more simply: " . . . to restore Verlaine to his state of child of the sun, was to restore the superiority that should have been his (understood on the poetic and spiritual level), to allow him to share the magic of the poet-seer" (*Oeuvres,* 552). Verlaine's hysteria, his mood swings, his alcoholism made him a dangerous companion, as Rimbaud often observed and confronted to his terror in Brussels.

The end of "Solde" is ambiguous:

—A vendre les Corps, les voix, l'immense opulence inquestionable,[8] ce qu'on ne vendra jamais. Les vendeurs ne sont pas à bout de solde! Les voyageurs n'ont pas à rendre leur commission de si tôt!

—For sale the Bodies, the voices, the immense unquestionable opulence, which will never be sold. The sellers aren't out of merchandise! The travelers won't have to turn over their commission for some time to come!

Guyaux comments on the way the anaphora undoes itself:

And the formula itself, breathless from repetition, loses its tone. It becomes its own negation. From now on it only denotes the absurd. *The sellers haven't sold out!* when it concerns *selling what can never be sold.* The anaphora is caught in its own trap: repetition produces the negation of what it continues to shout. . . . Finally, the word of the title, present in the orality of the second-to-last sentence, thereby expressing its very contradiction, reveals the spokenness of its object: *solde* is speech, a promise, like "For Sale," both speech and parody of the spoken word. (*Illuminations,* 271; emphasis in original)

Does Guyaux imply that Rimbaud becomes a ventriloquist for the world of commerce, selling only empty words? Or does he make the point that "Solde"'s irony turns on the fact that the great themes of poetry are not for sale? To me, "Solde" anticipates his strange words to Isabelle, a few days before he died: "Yes, they say they believe, but they only do it for the money." If there is "narcissistic gain" in the poem, it is at the expense of all the rhymesters and the "avachissement et gloire d'innombrables générations idiotes" ("the muck and glory of innumerable generations of idiots") that he savages in the "Lettre du voyant." Rimbaud stayed true to his original inspiration and in this late work (Guyaux places it last among the *Illuminations*) proudly confirms the fact that he never wrote for hire. There is bitterness and pride in "Solde," the ambivalence of a man who'd given everything that was best—his youth, his imagination, his passion—to an ephemeral and seemingly empty cause, poetry; and to a spineless lover, who'd proved unworthy of his devotion; and, as in so many other instances, there is prescience, as he looks ahead to a life on the road, a life of savage arguing over his accounts, until that last rendering with the Canon Chaulier in the Hôpital de la Conception in Marseilles.

VI

"His vision, his vision!"

14

Rimbaud's Ontology

"Villes II"

> Do we really know today the *horizon* that Rimbaud 'saw'? [. . .] Perhaps we can say this: the proximity of the *inaccessible* remains the region where only those rare beings who become poets arrive.
>
> —Martin Heidegger[1]

In an important book, first published in 1981, Marjorie Perloff named Rimbaud as initiator of "a poetics of indeterminacy," in which "the free play of possible significations replaces iconic representation."[2] The notion of the poem as enigma, in which signifier is detached from signified and word from referent, represents, in Perloff's view, a distinct lineage of High Modernism.

She summarizes the principal feature of this lineage as one in which: "forms can exist 'littéralement et dans tous les sens' ['literally and in all meanings'], an oscillation between representational reference and compositional game. To put it another way, William Empson's famous 'seven types of ambiguity,'—that is, the multiple layers of meaning words have in poetry (and by analogy, images in painting)—give way to what we might call an 'irreducible ambiguity'—the creation of labyrinths that have no exit" (34).

Perloff also makes this statement: " . . . the attempt to find consistent psychological themes in the *Illuminations* is repeatedly blocked." I think it is possible to show, as we have already seen in preceding chapters, that, while acknowledging an *apparent* cognitive indeterminacy of Rimbaud's *Illuminations,* we can also find a specific emotional quotient. Rimbaud's poems are always Barthesian "figures of desire." In "Villes II," Perloff's proof text, Rimbaud expresses the joy of poetic creation, "le plaisir du texte," with rhapsodic exuberance; but—to return to Perloff's central point—there is indeed a *cognitive* and *conceptual* obscurity that characterizes this poem. What I will attempt to show is that this indeterminacy or obscurity can be resolved by a radical change in perspective.

"Villes II"

"Villes II" opens: "Ce sont des villes! . . . " Perloff asks: "And where are we?" The description, she observes:

> . . . is neither that of a recognizable cityscape like Eliot's riverfront London [in *The Wasteland*] nor an ideal city of the imagination like Yeats' Byzantium. Rather, Rimbaud evokes "cities" that are, from the start, impossible to locate in "real" space. . . . In the course of the poem, the sense of place becomes more and more elusive . . . land and water finally merge in an hallucinatory image: the stags being suckled by Diana have their feet "in the waterfall and the brambles." From this point on, the mood of the poem becomes increasingly frenzied. (50, 51)

In conclusion, Perloff offers a statement from Todorov: "The *Illuminations* have established discontinuity as a fundamental rule. Rimbaud has made the absence of organization the principle of organization of these texts" (54, n13).

IF WE look for the reasons behind this turn toward obscurity in Rimbaud, I think the best way of accounting for it is by reference to the ontology of Martin Heidegger, who found in Western metaphysics a

> progressive masking or concealing of what was revealed in that *primordial experience*," i.e., the discovery of *physis* or being by the early Greeks.[3] Heidegger took as his philosophical task the unmasking of the substance ontology, that is, the view of reality as "what endures, what is permanent, what is always there. . . . To the extent that metaphysics focuses on 'beingness' and is blind to the conditions that let anything whatsoever show up, metaphysics has been dominated by 'error' or 'going astray.' . . . It follows, then, that the entire history of Western thought consists of variations on the initial answer to the question, What are entities? (18; emphasis added)

The issue for Heidegger—and for Rimbaud—is not what things are in and of themselves (the question of reference as posed by "indeterminacy")—but *how things are disclosed by consciousness*. And if Heidegger is to be our guide we will expect that things will become known in "the proximity of the inaccessible," that is, in a state of suspension between the seen and the unseen, the disclosed and the undisclosed.

We could then say that Rimbaud anticipated Heidegger, and gave us a poetry (the *Illuminations*) in which "entities" are put at question and their "way of showing up" becomes the real issue of the poems. Poems are not about things themselves but about how they are masked, revealed, transformed, recreated by consciousness.

Rimbaud's known is our unknown; his horizon is what we normally consider indeterminate or inaccessible. This is yet another way of reading the famous dictum: "Je est un autre / I is another!"[4] Rimbaud's pursuit of *Voyance* can be taken as the precursor of the course that led Heidegger to his attempt—both as arduous and conflicted as Rimbaud's poetics—to show how the being of entities is disclosed in *Dasein* (human consciousness).

How then does Rimbaud see "entities" and how does he enact their manner of presentation to consciousness?

In "Villes II" it isn't the "chalets de crystal / chalets of crystal" nor the "palmiers de cuivre / palm trees of copper" nor "les passerelles de l'abîme / the gangplanks of the abyss," etc., that are at issue, but rather how these images arise, how they surge into consciousness impelled by the mounting and descending rhythms of *poesis*. And concurrently, how do they reach us, act upon us, confuse or enlighten or motivate us? They are not grasped by the will to power but given in the "clearing" (*Lichtung*) of poetic consciousness.[5] Here they manifest what Heidegger calls "the Open of their paths." Meeting the resistance of the world, beings struggle for intimacy and, as they attain it in the poetic work, there occurs "the rise of the lighting of beings."[6]

Rimbaud's texts arise as seeming *non sequiturs,* as nonsense, as sparks of fire, as lies. . . . For after all, we live in a world of conventions determined by "the substance ontology"—often confusingly identified with "the metaphysic of presence."[7] However we may choose to reconfigure the poem, we know that we are reading words that are illusory; that, in other words, are referentially anomalous. Further, an emotional issue—*being lied to*—problematizes the way *knowing* takes place in Rimbaud's poems.

TO LEARN what Rimbaud thought of untruthfulness, our best document is "Les Poètes de sept ans"; and our best guide to that poem is Yves Bonnefoy's essay, "Madame Rimbaud."[8] Bonnefoy sums up his view of Rimbaud's mother in this way:

> Mme Rimbaud, in short, is one of the extreme examples, one of the most unbending, fanatical devotees of that cult of convention and propriety that has cast its shadow—and this is a lesson to be deeply pondered—over all realms formerly subject to the commandments of the law of love. In that very civilization that still pays lip service, at Charleville or elsewhere, to the God of the Incarnation, she stood as priestess, among a pious crowd, of a creed of excarnation, cold and gloomy as a crypt, which devotes life to the service of the law and finds its peculiar joy in thus reducing the unknown to the known, the inexhaustible to mere repetition. ("Madame Rimbaud," 72)

This then was the woman, the mother, who inspired Rimbaud's great poem, "Les Poètes de sept ans" where we find these lines:

> Pitié! ces enfants seuls étaient ses familiers
> Qui, chétifs, fronts nus, oeil déteignant sur la joue,
> Cachant des maigres doigts jaunes et noirs de boue
> Sous des habits puant la foire et tout vieillots,
> Conversaient avec la douceur des idiots!
> Et si, l'ayant surpris à des pitiés immondes,
> Sa mère s'effrayait; les tendresses profondes
> De l'enfant se jetaient sur cet étonnement.
> C'était bon. Elle avait le bleu regard, qui ment!

> Pity! Only those children were his friends
> Sickly kids, eyes draining on their cheek,
> Hiding thin fingers yellow black with mud
> Under worn-out shit-smelling clothes,
> Who talked with the gentleness of idiots!
> And if, catching him in acts of filthy pity,
> His mother took alarm; the deep tenderness
> Of the child fastened on that astonishment.
> So be it. She had the blue stare,—that lies!

Bonnefoy finds in these lines a crux of Rimbaud's childhood, recalled in this poem when he was seventeen. He thinks his mother must love him, because of her concern ("Sa mère s'effrayait / His mother was horrified"), but she removes him from these pitiable children for a reason that only *masquerades* as love. Bonnefoy writes: "But in fact, as Rimbaud realizes and must quickly have told himself, his mother is afraid only of bad examples in language or ideas that he may have acquired from his undesirable acquaintances, thus revealing yet again that what matters for her is her idea of what he ought to be, not what he is. . . . Her alarm, which ought to have implied love, was motivated solely by conventionality; and that is why her gaze is, as Rimbaud says, a 'lying' one" (79).

RIMBAUD'S AESTHETIC in the *Illuminations* is born in the blinding innocence of a child obliged to cope with his mother's lies. Her relationship to objects, to people, to society is determined by conventions that outlaw freedom, adventure and love; her *blue eyes that lie* project only a semblance of love, for she is motivated instead by propriety and *convenance*. He sets himself against her and all liars; this is first expressed in "La Lettre du voyant," where, astonishingly, he anticipates Heidegger: "Toute poésie antique aboutit à la poésie grecque. Vie harmonieuse.— De la Grèce au mouvement romantique,—moyen âge,—il y a des lettrés, des versificateurs / All the poetry of antiquity culminates in the poetry of Greece. Life in harmony.—From Greece to the romantic movement,—the middle ages,—there are only scholars, versifiers." What is wrong with these centuries of poetry? "Si les vieux imbéciles n'avaient pas trouvé du moi que la signification fausse, nous n'aurions pas à balayer ces millions de squelettes qui, depuis un temps infini, ont accumulé les produits de leur intelligence borgnesse, en s'en clamant les auteurs! / If those old imbeciles hadn't found only the false meaning of the self, we wouldn't have to sweep away these millions of skeletons that, since time immemorial, have accumulated the products of their stunted intelligence while acclaiming themselves the authors!" (*Oeuvres,* 363–64). A false view of the self (le moi) is to blame. Here, Rimbaud anticipates Heidegger's exploration of *Dasein* by the detour of his own determined search for truth, *Voyance*.

What the poet must do is exactly what Rimbaud set out to do during eight months or more when he tried to make his soul monstrous. *Voyance* was intended as an ascetic discipline, a reasoned detachment from his mother and her world; yet, at the same time, it was viewed and interpreted, by his mother and everyone else, as mere adolescent revolt. It served a double purpose: inner discipline on the one hand, outrage to his mother on the other.

This was a shrinking away of his whole being from her and the seeking of a new horizon, beyond which lay these stunning poems, the *Illuminations,* works that are in a certain sense "inaccessible" (as Heidegger calls that region known only to poets); but we need to narrow, as much as possible, the extent of that inaccessibility or indetermination. "Villes II," for example, is hermetic in image formation, but it arises out of a straightforward affective theme: "le plaisir du texte / textual pleasure." "Ce sont des villes! / These are cities!" is the opening line. It is like the "Fiat lux!" of *Genesis.* He is going to invent cities, a world. In the second sentence a similar indicative with imperative force creates people to inhabit these cities: "C'est un peuple pour qui se sont montés ces Alleghanys et ces Libans de rêve! / This is a people for whom these dream Alleghenies and Lebanons have arisen!" Isn't this exactly what Barthes calls "a paradise of words"?[9]

The emotional force in "Villes II" is a fundamental aesthetic pleasure in the joy of creation, the joy of a virtuoso exploring the resources of his instrument. But there is a further answer to the question about referentiality, i.e., about the cognitive meaning of the display of extravagant descriptive images, following one another in serial fashion, that structures the poem. In these cities, there are celebrations ("des fêtes amoureuses / amorous festivals") and catastrophes ("l'écroulement des apothéoses / the collapse of apotheoses"); divine birth ("la naissance éternelle de Vénus / the eternal birth of Venus") and orphic sounds ("[les] flottes orphéoniques et ... la rumeur des perles et de conques précieuses / orpheonic fleets and ... the rumble of pearls and of precious shells"). Varying genealogies of fairies appear ("Des cortèges de Mabs") along with goddesses ("Vénus and Diana"). As in "Le Bateau ivre," there are symphonies of sound: "Les Bacchantes des banlieues sanglotent et la lune brûle et hurle / The Bacchantes of the suburbs sob and the moon burns and screams"). Following the lead of Baudelaire, Rimbaud saw the city as the privileged capital of all that was modern and desirable in contemporary life. And there is an echo of the ending of *Une Saison en enfer,* where he imagines himself, together with a chosen companion: "Et à l'aurore, armés d'une ardente patience, nous entrerons aux splendides villes / And at dawn, armed with an ardent patience, we will enter the splendid cities." These cities are the site of poetic imagination, where Rimbaud takes the path that Heidegger called "letting things come into the openness of human existence as they are."[10] Not as things are given by convention but as they surge up in poetic expressivity. Rimbaud's use of the city anticipates Heidegger's evocation of the Greek temple in his essay on "The Origin of the

Work of Art." Rimbaud too yearns for a symbol that "gathers around the unity of those paths and relations in which birth and death, disaster and blessing, victory and disgrace, endurance and decline, acquire the shape of destiny for human Being."[11] This is how "Villes II" (or any great work of art) articulates a culture, manifests the world.[12]

To create a city, as Rimbaud does in his two poems entitled "Villes," is to challenge death, even while he foresees the horizon of his own death. In the poem death is a "present-at-hand" reality, out there, just beyond the horizon. At the same time, his transformational poetics, while it evokes a place of every dream and desire, allows him to postpone the one truth that he cannot doubt—the fact that he will die at a particular moment, in one particular place—a place that is not among the "châteaux bâtis en os / chateaux built from bones" or among the "fabuleux fantômes des monts / fabulous phantoms of mountains" that occur in "Villes II." These magical places are within the poem's horizon; the region of death lies beyond. So his creation of the city includes all those places where he will not yet have to die.

The poem ends with a question: "Quels bons bras, quelle belle heure me rendront cette région d'où viennent mes sommeils et mes moindres mouvements? / What fond arms, what fine hour will return to me that region where arise my sleeps and my least movements?" All his life Rimbaud searched for those arms, that presence, that "other" who would return his love and restore his dreams ("mes sommeils"). This poignant question evokes the realm not only of sleep but of life itself—("mes moindres mouvements")—the circulation of his blood, the beating of his heart, the nervous impulses that control his muscles. Within the circumscription of this desire for love, for holding, for nurture, the adumbrations of his dreams and desires arise; and from them arise the evanescent cities of his poems. Even had he known that love, those arms, he could never have imagined the finale awaiting him at l'Hôpital de la Conception in Marseilles.

"VILLES II" is an alternate world of beauty and mystery set against the conventional "substance ontology" of Madame Rimbaud, who embodied that stance to a grotesque degree. Not only did Rimbaud react against his mother's lies, *he told lies of his own.* He too had blue eyes—that lie. Rimbaud fuses her dishonesty with his own poetic talent and proves he can tell far better lies than she can. His lies become poetry and manifest a world where everything is different from the "cosmorama Arduan," as he describes his home in the Ardennes (*Oeuvres*, 369). He systematically sets out to undo his mother's inauthentic vision of things and prove that everything is different. We know that on one occasion Mme Rimbaud read some of *Une Saison en enfer* and, bewildered, asked him what it meant. His reply was, "It means exactly what it says." In other words, these *lies and distortions* are my truth: the truth that arises in the mind of genius when it can escape the boundaries of conventional reference and, in total freedom, let new worlds be.

15

Sublimation in
Une Saison en enfer

To take up again the Rimbaud/Verlaine saga, let us recall the date of early April 1872, when Rimbaud, full of anger, wrote "Honte / Shame." Not long after that, Verlaine called him back to Paris where he spent a summer of solitary drunkenness, "made to feel," Petitfils writes, "that he was in quarantine, like some plague victim" (146). He wrote very little. The summer was stifling. Deciding he'd had enough, he hand-carried a letter to Verlaine, saying he was leaving for Antwerp. He met Verlaine on the way, going out to fetch a doctor for his wife who was ill. Verlaine blurted out: "I'll go with you!" They conferred hastily. It would be Brussels, not Antwerp. To fund this escapade, Verlaine would tell his mother that he was threatened with arrest for having been a Communard; she would give him money.[1]

Mathilde, Verlaine's wife, followed him to Brussels; there were horrible scenes and a police report that called Rimbaud "a monster." Eventually, Verlaine chose freedom from a job he hated as well as from his wife and child; on September 7, 1872 the two poets sailed for England.

UNE SAISON EN ENFER is dated April–August 1873. It was begun in Roche in April, entitled at that point "Livre païen / Pagan Book" or "Livre nègre / Negro Book." Rimbaud was deeply invested in his literary career and he wrote Delahaye, à propos this work in progress, "Mon sort dépend de ce livre. / My fate depends on this book."

Une Saison is not a seamless work, but it has proven impossible to date and identify the various segments. A sketch by Verlaine titled "Comment se fit la *Saison en enfer* / How *Season in Hell* was written" shows Rimbaud in a London public house working on the manuscript. This is a second stage in the book's development. What had begun in Roche as a series of "histoires atroces / atrocious stories" became in "Mauvais Sang" a frantic search for identity that seems discontinuous with later segments.

In London the couple's existence, never idyllic, became more fraught and it was almost impossible for either to work. There were violent quarrels, drunken rages, often they came to blows. Terrified of legal proceedings undertaken by his wife, Verlaine was hysterical. Mathilde Mauté was asking for separation on ten grounds, including acts of violence perpetrated against her; also desertion, and homosexuality. Rimbaud was deeply involved in all this. Petitfils writes:

> At this time, therefore, Rimbaud was partly aware at least that the experiment [to make Verlaine "un fils du soleil"] had failed. It was a failure of which he would be the principal victim, for he would not go unscathed by that legal business: in accusing Verlaine of having run away with a young man, Mathilde was aiming at him, and her lawyers would unmask him; the authorities would probably intervene, since he was still a minor. Inevitably, one day or another, his mother would learn of the unspeakable insinuations being leveled at him. On top of everything else, it would be the ruin of his literary career. (162)

The strain became unbearable and on July 3, 1873, Verlaine abandoned London and fled back to Brussels, hoping that his wife would join him. But in fact he would never see her again. It was Rimbaud, penniless and abandoned, who made the trip to Brussels. It was there, despite the presence of Verlaine's mother, that the relationship degenerated into a violent argument, provoked by Rimbaud's stubborn insistence on returning to Paris. The drunken Verlaine, who had bought a revolver to commit suicide, fired two shots at his companion, wounding Arthur in the left wrist.[2] Out on the street Verlaine threatened Rimbaud again and was arrested by a policeman. Rimbaud was briefly hospitalized, Verlaine was booked on a charge of assault and sentenced to eighteen months in prison. After those decisive events Rimbaud returned to Roche and threw himself with new energy into what now became *Une Saison en enfer*. His brush with death is the crux around which the entire work implicitly turns. This incident, not part of the original plan, accounts for the sense of catastrophe that hangs over the work like a black cloud. And there is Rimbaud's own guilt for Verlaine's situation—his insistence on returning to Paris, then the call for help that provoked his friend's arrest.

The act of violence was the climax of a relationship that dominated Rimbaud's life for two years. His finest poetry was written with Verlaine serving as both inspiration and mentor.[3] Rimbaud reached sexual maturity in this relationship, which brought him both intense rewards and a commensurate sense of degradation. It is no wonder, then, that his whole life, past, present and future, is distilled into the work that he wrote while still under the emotional influence of that season in hell. André Guyaux finds the work "grandiloquent"; Paul Valéry belittled the work's style: "It consists only of direct statements, ejaculations, intensity."[4] The strongest negative judgment of *Une Saison* is that of Leo Bersani: "The *Saison* is a desperate and confused surrender to the inevitability of both personal and cultural history. The very repudiation of the past is an act which *gives* a significant past to Rimbaud" (emphasis in original). He adds, "But in *Une Saison en enfer,* Rimbaud's repudiations of his past are made in a language which undermines the effectiveness of the repudiations themselves" (*Astyanax,* 238).

In my view, Rimbaud is not "repudiating" his past in *Une Saison,* nor is he trying to justify it; he is too honest for both those forms of self-delusion. Rather, he is restaging that past in imagination, trying, first, to understand its deeper meaning, and second, recast it in a form that will reconcile him with some version of moral rectitude and allow self-acceptance. Although the work may at moments appear chaotic, it is nonetheless powerfully directed toward a cathartic outcome.

Given the various negative evaluations of the book, I want to pose two questions: What is the form of *Une Saison en enfer,* a book that has too often been seen as chaotic and confused? And then, what psychic process is at work here, giving—indeed *mandating*—the form that the work possesses?

IN HIS STUDY of the *Saison,* Yves Bonnefoy claims that the poet is writing only for himself: "He must find himself, collect himself, proffer to his will a pact for years to come, and someone who writes under such severe constraints does not consider how he will be read" (111). Certainly Rimbaud is writing out of his own deep distress and a corrosive guilt; but it is impossible to ignore the fact that he had become a pariah, despised by the Parisian literary world as principal cause of the breakup of Verlaine's marriage and imprisonment. Already in London the exiled communards sniggered at their relationship. After Verlaine's departure, Rimbaud went to visit Jules Andrieu, a man he admired, and was roughly thrown out of the house in front of witnesses (Petitfils, 174).

When he returned to Paris, hoping to win recognition for *Une Saison,* he found that he was far better known for his adventures with Verlaine than for his poetry. People refused to associate with him, and, some months later in July 1873, when Germain Nouveau went to London with Rimbaud, Nouveau's friends expressed consternation and warned him of disastrous consequences.

Rimbaud is writing for himself, but this apologia is also directed at the society he affected to despise because it had rejected him. Rimbaud wants to have mastery over his life, but instead he has encountered his own nullity, the fact that he almost died—and that one day he will die. For the first time in his life Rimbaud, at age nineteen, must face the inevitability of death.[5]

In *Une Saison* he is asking himself why everything in his life has gone so disastrously wrong and what he can do to redeem himself in his own eyes and in the eyes of the world. He is both confronting his experience and sublimating it; that is, in the words of Hans Loewald, reconciling "on a higher level of organization, the early magic of thought, gesture, word, image emotion, fantasy." He is recasting as a cultural (and hence socially acceptable) artifact the instinctual drives that empowered him during those wild and intoxicating years with Verlaine (Loewald, 80–81).

The months spent writing *Une Saison en enfer* represent a period during which Rimbaud undertook his own psychotherapy; and it is in this work that we find the rudiments of a Rimbaldian psychology.[6] The path he charts for himself is not based on "a psychotechnology for self improvement" (Guignon, 220), but rather in the search for a new life, based on commitment to a radically different future that recuperates the mistakes and failures of the past. Not only does he accept sublimation and repression ("pas une main d'ami / no friendly hand"), but he can honestly accept his homosexuality, bringing to bear a clear-sighted lucidity that condemns him to a lonely existence, outside the social norms of his time and place.

SUBLIMATION in the *Saison* occurs under the guise of fiction, but it is never given the substitutive value that sublimation attains in Proust. Leo

Bersani writes of the redemptive role of art in Proust, where the art we prize requires a devaluation of the very life out of which it arises. Proust represents an extreme case of the depreciation of life against art. Bersani summarizes Proust's aesthetic, "Experience destroys; art restores" (14).

While Bersani sees Proustian sublimation as repression and loss, Loewald makes the case that sublimation is "a separation that is not a separation but a form of union, a reconciliation of polarities" (23). The cultural product or symbol (the transitional object) redeems the trauma of the separation of infant and mother. In other words, Proust's vast work becomes the symbol in which he restores "lost time," i.e., the time of the child's separation from his mother. Sublimation, therefore, is not tragic because through it separation is magically healed. Bersani argues that the notion of redemption (i.e., healing, restoring) through art is excessive in the case of Proust and also in Rimbaud's *Une Saison en enfer.*

IN *UNE SAISON* ellipsis and understatement replace representation. Instead of the inflating Proustian sublime, Rimbaud's tone is ironical and deflating. In sharply controlled sentences, Rimbaud details the three major failures of his life: failure of the *Voyance* experiment; failure of his effort "to reinvent love"; and finally, related to the second point, the failure of his relationship with Verlaine. After Brussels he returns to Roche, shuts himself up in the attic, and attempts to write his way out of this triple impasse. The "way out" is sublimation; and it takes the form of the rhetorical figure known as chiasmus, based on the Greek letter X, chi. Chiasmus is a dynamic arrangement of two sets of terms that press against each other and seek to cross or change places. It can be represented by the formula ABBA. The *Saison* involves a struggle to formulate the problem of happiness in this trope where good A—A' subdues evil BB'. The problem to be resolved is the *transformation* of youthful happiness across degradation and back into moral worth.

UNE SAISON is composed of a preface followed by eight parts. There is an internal logic and the progressive unfolding of an argument. Rimbaud is using his considerable poetic and intellectual gifts to argue his case before a hostile public. He argues that he is not a reprobate, a demon, a *rejeton* who should be cast into the bonfire. He needs to convince us that, though he has passed through hell, he should not be condemned to stay there. *Sublimation* is implied by the fact that he feels the need to plead his case. While this goes on, there is a back current of desublimation, in which he expresses his anger, frustration, and aggression. It comes out most openly in "Délires I, Vierge folle," at the midpoint of the work, where he punishes Verlaine in a blistering parody, the product of rage too long contained.

The work begins with a series of metonymic terms for lost childhood happiness, ending with the wine metaphor: "Jadis, si je me souviens bien, ma vie était un festin où s'ouvraient tous les coeurs, où tous les vins coulaient." To sit Beauty on his lap like a child continues the metonymic chain, but because the speaker is no longer a child, no longer participant in the feast, he feels bitterness and anger:

> Un soir, j'ai assis la Beauté sur mes genoux.—Et je l'ai trouvée amère.—
>   Et je l'ai injuriée.
> Je me suis armé contre la justice.
> Je me suis enfui. O sorcières, ô misère, ô haine, c'est à vous que mon
>   trésor a été confié!

> One evening, I sat Beauty on my knees.—But I found her bitter.—and I
>   cursed her.
> I took arms against justice.
> I fled. O witches, O poverty, O hate, it's to you that I have confided my
>   treasure!

Lawler argues that *Les Fleurs du mal* was Rimbaud's immediate model. The parallel with Baudelaire is apparent; but it is important to insist that the Christianity of Baudelaire was conventional; that is, Baudelaire believed in God, he considered himself a sinner,[7] while Rimbaud had undergone the influence of persuasive anticlerical thinkers such as Helvetius, d'Holbach, Michelet, and Renan. Moreover, as a homosexual, Rimbaud felt himself excluded from the Christian communion by the doctrine of natural law.[8]

His childhood memories are laced with ceremonies, once embraced, which now he sees as priestcraft and superstition. And he'll remember whispered confessions to a grim profile behind the grill of the confessional, parodied in his avowal to witches, to poverty, and to hatred. In Michelet's book, *La Sorcière*, the witch becomes symbolic of all who are rejected by the social order. Those lost souls are, as Rimbaud knows himself to be, pariahs. Yet he has swung the censer to honor the Blessed Sacrament; he has prayed Novenas and knelt before the statue of the Blessed Virgin; he has fasted and huddled on bruised knees while the celebrant walks up and down the aisle sprinkling holy water and blessing the parishioners. On Ash Wednesday he has felt the priest's thumb scrape his forehead with ashes and intone: "Memento, homo, quia pulvus es et in pulverem revertetis / Remember, man, you are dust and to dust you shall return." When you have lived all this for your first fifteen years of life, it is in the proteins of your brain, it is engraved on your soul forever.

THIS PREFACE to the poem proper breaks neatly in two. The first section runs from "Jadis" to "folie." It is a succinct account of the joys of childhood and the horrors of his adolescent revolt after he found Beauty to be bitter. The second section begins with his brush with death—the two shots from Verlaine's revolver: "Or, tout dernièrement m'étant trouvé sur le point de faire le dernier *couac! / But, quite recently, on the verge of giving my last croak!*" Here the tone is ironic, self-mocking. In that instant, during the struggle in the hotel room, the two shots from Verlaine's revolver bring the nineteen-year-old Rimbaud face to face with his own death. At this point Rimbaud avoids the realization that death is constant and all-pervasive; instead, he turns back and tries vainly to reinvent his childhood joys: "Or, tout dernièrement... j'a songé à rechercher la clef du festin ancien, où je reprendrais peut-être appétit." He finds that the key to lost happiness is just what the Church says it is—*charity*. "Cette inspiration prouve que j'ai rêvé! / That inspiration proves that I've been dreaming!" When you have luxuriated in mortal sin, when you have denied God's love, when you have betrayed your baptismal vows, there's no going back. Satan judges him irrevocably lost: "Tu restera hyène.../ You'll remain a hyena...."

Rimbaud is afflicted with some of his mother's Jansenism. He doesn't think he can regain God's grace; or maybe he doesn't want to. Baudelaire, who had known a mother's love, could live in the Church.[9] Rimbaud, rejected by his mother, alienated by his very sexuality, could not.

"Mauvais sang"

"Mauvais sang," the first of the six sections, asks the question: "Who am I?" He is proud to claim a Gallic heritage:

> Les Gaulois étaient les écorcheurs de bêtes, les brûleurs d'herbes les
>   plus ineptes de leur temps.

D'eux j'ai: l'idolâtrie et l'amour du sacrilège;—oh! tous les vices, colère, luxure,—magnifique, la luxure;—surtout mensonge et paresse.

The Gauls were flayers of beasts, and the most inept grass burners of their time.
From them I get: idolatry and love of sacrilege;—oh! all the vices, anger, lust,—magnificent, lust;—but especially deceit and sloth.

Here he seems to parade his sexuality (luxure), to take pride in it; but there is a move toward sublimation nonetheless. He gives it a genetic origin: he can't deny his heritage! Back there in Paris, when he behaved in uncouth fashion, when people saw him as a loutish peasant, he was simply acknowledging his origins.¹⁰

There follows a long passage of denials. He lists all the things he is not: not an aristocrat but a primitive. Uncivilized, perhaps the lowest laborer in a Crusader caravan, not even a Christian but a superstitious changeling dancing a witches' Sabbath.

The antithesis to the above is a paean to science: "Oh! la science!" Here is the avowal of Rimbaud's commitment to "social illuminism," the belief that modern science (the substitute religion of Michelet and Quinet) will unlock the wonders of the universe and bring eventual freedom to all mankind. "La science, la nouvelle noblesse! Le progrès . . . / Science, the new nobility! Progress . . . " But what does this have to do with the sins for which he is on trial? Implicit in the paean to science is the understanding that, in a truly modern society, homosexuality will be acceptable, the invert will not be exposed and humiliated.

After "science" he reasserts his paganism:

Le sang païen revient! L'Esprit est proche, pourquoi Christ ne m'aide-t-il pas, en donnant à mon âme noblesse et liberté. Hélas! l'Evangile a passé! l'Evangile! l'Evangile!

My pagan blood returns! The Spirit is near, Why doesn't Christ help me, by giving my soul nobility and freedom. Alas! the Gospel has gone by! the Gospel! the Gospel!

After he left Verlaine, penitent and converted in a Belgian prison, Rimbaud himself thought of conversion. On the back of the drafts of *Une Saison* are scenes from the Gospel of Saint John. These show the influence of Renan's *Vie de Jésus* and are parodic and ironical. He wavers, now invoking the Gospel and the Holy Spirit, now reverting to sarcasm and sacrilege. His comment on those Gospel sketches is: "*De profundis, Domine,* suis-je bête! / *De profundis,* Lord, how stupid I am!"[11] Also in "Mauvais Sang" he writes sarcastically: "Je ne me crois pas embarqué pour une noce avec Jésus-Christ pour beau-père / I don't consider myself embarked for a wedding with Jesus Christ as father-in-law." D. W. Winnicott speaks of a patient who experienced an "unpredictable compulsion to blaspheme against the Holy Ghost." Rimbaud's blasphemy is a common reaction to early religious indoctrination; but he resembles Winnicott's patient in another respect: he suffers "from an environmental pattern in which the inadequacy was of the nature of a weak [or absent] father and a strong mother" (Winnicott, 236). Even when we take into account Rimbaud's real problems with nineteenth-century French Catholicism, we need to remember that "the inverted Oedipus complex" (strong mother, absent father) is everywhere in *Une Saison en enfer.*

RIMBAUD'S UNCLE was called "L'Africain," because he had spent many years as a soldier in Africa before returning to assume control of the family farm. Whatever Rimbaud's relationship may have been with this taciturn and withdrawn man, the vision of the dark continent as a possible escape hatch always intrigued him:

> Oui, j'ai les yeux fermés à votre lumière. Je suis une bête, un nègre. Mais je puis être sauvé. Vous êtes de faux nègres, vous maniaques, féroces, avares... Le plus malin est de quitter ce continent où la folie rôde pour pourvoir d'otages ces misérables. J'entre au vrai royaume des enfants de Cham.

> Yes, my eyes are shut to your light. I'm a beast, a negro. But I can be saved. You are fake negroes, you maniacs, killers, usurers.... My best bet is to leave this continent where madness lurks to provide these wretches with hostages. I'm entering the true kingdom of the children of Ham.

Throughout "Mauvais Sang" the speaker imagines himself in roles that set him apart and make him dramatically different from his family, his countrymen—the "vous" to whom the poem is addressed.

This monologue, Rimbaud's "examen de conscience," is driven by a furious dialectic. Though many steps in the dialectic are elided, he arrives at an exculpatory (if only provisional) conclusion:

> La raison m'est née. Le monde est bon. Je bénirai la vie. J'aimerai mes frères. Ce ne sont plus des promesses d'enfance. Ni l'espoir d'échapper à la vieillesse et à la mort. Dieu fait ma force, et je loue Dieu.
>
> Reason is born in me. The world is good. I will bless life. I'll love my brothers. These are no longer a child's promises. Nor the hope of escaping old age and death. God gives me strength and I praise God.

But this is all phony, the same "false conversion" he attributes to Verlaine. The dialectic drives on and he finds himself playing cowboy and Indian with the Devil. The next section is "Nuit de l'enfer" ("Night of hell"). Here *Une Saison en enfer* reaches a feverish crescendo of conflicting emotions.

"Nuit de l'enfer"

There are several views of "une fameuse gorgée de poison / a famous mouthful of poison" in the first line of "Nuit de l'enfer." But the "mouthful of poison" can only mean one thing—baptism. A born and bred Catholic like Rimbaud understands that baptism entitles you to heaven; if rejected, baptism makes you a prime candidate for hell. And (though he had "entrevu la conversion au bien et au bonheur . . . des millions de créatures charmantes, un suave concert spirituel . . . / half-seen the conversion to goodness and happiness . . . millions of charming creatures, an exquisite spiritual concert . . . ") it is given that he will choose hell. Why? Out of pride. "*Orgueil.*" The word is isolated; it blocks all the charming images of salvation ("Ah! l'enfance, l'herbe, la pluie, le lac sur les pierres, le clair de lune quand le clocher sonnait douze . . . / Ah! childhood, grass, the rain, the lake over the pebbles, the moonlight when the bell-tower struck midnight . . . "). But the devil is in the bell-tower. "Nuit de l'enfer" involves a subtle form of sublimation. He hides his sense of guilt through mockery. He is an Inquisitor conducting his own *auto-da-fé*. Making accomplices of his readers, he invites them to enjoy the torments of his "sosie," his double, a not entirely fictitious character:

> Ah! remonter à la vie! Jeter les yeux sur nos difformités. Et ce poison, ce baiser mille fois maudit! Ma faiblesse, la cruauté du monde! Mon Dieu, pitié, cachez-moi, je me tiens trop mal!—Je suis caché et je ne le suis pas.
>
> C'est le feu qui se relève avec son damné.

> Ah! to rise again to life! To cast eyes upon our deformities. And that poison, that kiss a thousand times accursed! My weakness, the cruelty of the world! Dear God, have pity, hide me, I'm losing control!—I'm hidden and in plain sight.
>
> It is the fire that rises with its damned one.

The poet is ostensibly telling us what it feels like to be damned; but his emotional template for damnation is that horrible moment, back in the hotel room, when Verlaine fired two shots from his revolver. Rimbaud writes of the emotions he felt when Verlaine backed him up against the wall, pointed the revolver at him, and shouted, "Je t'apprendrai à vouloir partir! / I'll teach you to try and leave!"

SINCE EVERYTHING in *Une Saison en enfer* is antithetical to something else, we should ask here: what is the antithesis to death and damnation? Here we encounter the poem's central chiasmus.

In his searching essay on sublimation, Bersani refers to the "attachment of the ego to its own moral worth" (*Redemption*, 38). But what are the criteria for "moral worth"? It is clear that the implicit values of nineteenth-century bourgeois morality form the background against which Rimbaud enacts the drama of his "trial" for moral turpitude and general unworthiness. But these are not his values; for in rejecting the Church, Rimbaud also rejected the "substance ontology" that he had learned as a child. Nothing is given a priori and genius is no excuse in this court, whoever the masked judge may be—Satan or God himself.

Try as he will—by dialectic, casuistry, role playing—he can't convince the "judge" of his innocence. And again, who is the judge? It is the communards in London who snickered at the two lovers, it is Mathilde Mauté (Verlaine's wife) and her lawyers, it is (God forbid!) his mother.[12] But first and foremost, it is Rimbaud himself. This is the moment when Rimbaud begins to understand that moral worth does not preexist, and that is why it eludes him. *He must define his own moral worth.* If Rimbaud starts at A—Salvation and then, as he crosses the space of the chiasmus, encounters B, B'—death and damnation, how can he be sure that, if he seeks farther along this perilous path, he will find A' or moral worth? To open and successfully close the chiasmus is to risk everything on a roll of the dice.

Chiasmus is dynamic: the two inner terms (B, B') press outward against the enclosing terms (A, A') that press inward with only a slightly superior force. Or, to put this in Freudian terms, the chiasmus enacts the return of the repressed. What he has repressed (anger, fear, violence) [B, B'] must be held in check by the countervailing force of sublimation [A, A']. Ultimately, of course, there must be a spiritual process that neutralizes BB' and provides stasis, rest, peace, self-acceptance, reconciliation.

"Délires I"

"Délires I/Delirium I," "Vierge folle/Foolish virgin," stages Verlaine's plea of nonresponsibility. He tells the Lord that he couldn't help himself, that he was induced to sin by the wiles of "L'Epoux infernal / the infernal Husband." We are in a courtroom, where a weeping pederast is casting blame on his juvenile sexual partner:

> —Lui était presque un enfant. . . . Ses délicatesses mystérieuses m'avaient séduite. J'ai oublié tout mon devoir humain pour le suivre. Quelle vie! La vraie vie est absente. Nous ne sommes pas au monde. Je vais où il va, il le faut. Et souvent il s'emporte contre moi, *moi, la pauvre âme*. Le Démon!—C'est un Démon, vous savez, *ce n'est pas un homme.*

> —He was still a child. . . . His mysterious delicate ways seduced me. I neglected my every human duty to follow him. What a life! Real life is somewhere else. We are not in the world. I go where he goes, I must. And often he flies into a rage at *me, poor me*. The Demon! He's a Demon, you know, *he's not a man.* (emphasis in original)

Rimbaud expertly mixes comedy and pathos, and in the process, as Lawler remarks, parodies the very style of Verlaine in such books as *Poèmes saturniens* and *Romances sans paroles.*

How can you blame either of us? Rimbaud implies, it was all such a foolish mistake. My grandiosity, his obsequious devotion—neither of us is to be taken seriously! We were caught up in a delirium brought on by absinthe and subversive books. The intense relationship between the two, with all its ecstasy and madness, is reduced to the stand-up comedy of a drag queen. There is not just comedy here but pathos. We have only to remember Rimbaud's letter from London begging Verlaine to return:

> Reviens, reviens, cher ami, seul ami, reviens. Je te jure que je serai bon. Si j'étais maussade avec toi, c'est une plaisanterie où je me suis entêté, je m'en repens plus qu'on ne peut dire. Reviens, ce sera bien oublié. Quel

malheur que tu aies cru à cette plaisanterie. Voilà deux jours que je ne cesse de pleurer . . .

Come back, come back, dear friend, only friend, come back. I swear that I'll be good. If I was sulky with you, it was a stubborn joke, I'm more sorry than I can say. Come back, forget it. What a shame you took that joke seriously. I've been crying for two days . . . (Pléiade, 170)

This was an authentic passion, expressed also in Rimbaud's poetry, in the complex alembics of "Dévotion" as Lawler has skillfully revealed or in the tenderness of "Vagabonds." Yet here, at the heart of his great confessional poem, that passion is parodied and given its *coup de grâce*. Rimbaud never again took Verlaine seriously, though, throughout the years that followed, "le pauvre Lelian" (anagram of Paul Verlaine) continued to publish and praise the younger "poète maudit."[13]

"Délires II"

"Délires II," "Alchimie du verbe / Alchemy of the word" is another matter. Here Rimbaud gives a magical mystery tour of his experiment in *Voyance*. There are also lyrics of casual beauty, "vieilleries poétiques / poetic antiquities"—inn signboards, church Latin, fairy tales, old operas, naïve rhymes—evoking times past or eternity. They do not involve sublimation so we shall pass over them.

"L'Impossible"

The next section, "L'Impossible," opens with recall of a past joy that he was too inexperienced to recognize:

Ah! cette vie de mon enfance, la grande route par tous les temps, sobre surnaturellement, plus désintéressé que le meilleur des mendiants, fier de n'avoir ni pays, ni amis, quelle sottise c'était.—Et je m'en aperçois seulement!

Ah! that life of my childhood, the highway in all weather, supernaturally sober, more disinterested than the best of beggars, proud to have neither country nor friends, what madness it was.—And I realize it only now!

Then he looks at his present state, the company he keeps—they are all people he despises! "J'ai eu raison dans tous mes dédains: puisque je m'évade! / I was right in all my disdains: since I'm escaping!" Guided by intuition, by feeling alone, he takes the cue to cut and run:

> Hier encore, je soupirais: "Ciel! sommes-nous assez de damnés ici-bas! Moi j'ai tant de temps déjà dans leur troupe! Je les connais tous. Nous nous reconnaissons toujours; nous nous dégoûtons. La charité nous est inconnue. Mais nous sommes polis; nos relations avec le monde sont très-convenables."

> Only yesterday, I was sighing: "Heavens! there are enough of us damned souls down here! Myself I've spent too much time in their troop! I know them all. We always recognize each other: we disgust one another. Charity is unknown to us. But we're polite; our relations with other people are very-correct."

He's dividing society into us and them—the poets and artists vs. the *bons bourgeois*. All that can be said for his "troop" is that they have good manners. Polite, correct, but without charity. But who am I kidding, he seems to say; the believers, the churchgoers aren't any better. Can it be that "moral worth" is a chimera, out of reach for all of us? Once again Rimbaud is driven to situate himself, to find the place in the moral universe where he belongs; but, no matter how the monologue twists and turns, he can never rid himself of a sense of guilt.[14] Enough of that! He's talking like a moralist, one of those *raisonneurs* of the eighteenth century.

"Mais je m'aperçois que mon esprit dort. / But I realize that my mind is asleep." And this admission provides a bridge to truth:

> S'il était bien éveillé toujours à partir de ce moment nous serions bientôt à la vérité, qui peut-être nous entoure avec ses anges pleurant! . . . —S'il avait été éveillé jusqu'à ce moment-ci, c'est que je n'aurais pas cédé aux instincts délétères, à une époque immémoriale! . . . —S'il avait toujours été bien éveillé, je voguerais en pleine sagesse! . . .
>
> O pureté! pureté!
>
> C'est cette minute d'éveil qui m'a donné la vision de la pureté!—Par l'esprit on va à Dieu!
>
> Déchirante infortune!

> If it were awake then from that moment on, we would be in the truth,

that perhaps surrounds us with its weeping angels! . . . —If it had been awake up to this very minute, I would not have given in to deleterious instincts in a time now past! . . . —If it had always been awake, I would sail in full wisdom! . . .

O purity! purity!

It's this minute of awareness which has given me the vision of purity!—By the spirit one goes to God!

Agonizing misfortune!

Rimbaud is momentarily entrapped by what Valéry called sarcastically his "jaculations"—not simply cries or exclamations but bursts of pious fervor. Here the syntax wraps around itself; he gives up the disguise that sublimation entails and confronts his weakness and moral flaws head on. His defensive irony fails, he speaks the truth when he says: "Agonizing misfortune!"

I can't help but agree with Claudel, who saw *Une Saison* as "an incomparable document," ennobled by its very defects, as in the stuttering passage cited above.

For a Catholic, "purity" is a sexual reference; and here we are reminded of how bitterly Rimbaud resented his sexual orientation and blamed it for the misadventures of his life. Lawler sees the "impossible" of the title as a reference to the blockage of reason. I see this "Déchirante infortune" as the cry of a nineteenth-century homosexual who laments the impossibility of ever experiencing a socially acceptable form of love. What had begun as a reasoned critique of Western culture (at worst a brash undertaking for a nineteen-year-old) becomes a pathetic expression of remorse. There is a brusque emotional reversal and a consequent desublimation that subverts the original intent of the section. That is to say, he had attacked the womanizers, rakes, and pimps; but now it is his own lack of purity that is at issue. He can never be a blameless spirit.

"L'Eclair"

"Le travail humain! C'est l'explosion qui éclaire mon abîme de temps en temps."

("Human work! It's the explosion that lights up my abyss from time to time.")

Critic Mario Matucci suggests that Rimbaud sees work as expiation for his almost twenty years of wasted life. Everybody keeps shouting "Work!

work!" In fact, it is Madame Rimbaud who has been preaching work to him for as long as he can remember. Sitting in his attic in Roche writing *Une Saison en enfer*, Rimbaud heard repeatedly from his mother that he should learn a trade, be useful; that he should take part in the planting and the harvesting of the crops. Under maternal pressure he considers the merits of work as opposed to scribbling all day long.

There is violence, impatience, self-contradiction in this section made of stops and starts: "Ah! vite, vite un peu; là-bas, par delà la nuit, ces récompenses futures, éternelles . . . les échappons-nous? . . . " ("Ah! quick, quick; over there, beyond the night, those future, eternal rewards . . . will we miss out on them?").

"La mother" has often chastised him about the danger of losing his immortal soul. "Qu'y puis-je? / What can I do?" he answers her: "Je connais le travail; et la science est trop lente / I know work; and science is too slow." In a tormented dialogue with his super-ego, Rimbaud produces one phony excuse after another:

> Ma vie est usée. Allons! feignons, fainéantons, ô pitié! Et nous existerons en nous amusant, en rêvant amours monstres et univers fantastiques, en nous plaignant et en querellant les apparences du monde, saltimbanque, mendiant, artiste, bandit, prêtre! Sur mon lit d'hôpital, l'odeur de l'encens m'est revenue si puissante; gardien des aromates sacrés, confesseur, martyr . . .

> My life is used up. Come! pretend, let's be idle, O pity! And we'll exist by having fun, in dreaming monstrous loves, in complaining and arguing about fantastic worlds, clown, beggar, artist, bandit, priest! On my hospital bed, the odor of incense, so overpowering, came back to me; guardian of the sacred ointments, confessor, martyr . . .

Suddenly, out of nowhere, comes a memory of l'Hôpital Saint-Jean in Brussels. Regression to infancy at a time of sickness is a common experience; but why should he recall the Catholic Church, which he has renounced and now despises? The Church that, furthermore, was associated with his pious, bigoted mother. Clearly, his years as a young acolyte in the Church have left their mark. Here, the sacramental (incense) is a screen memory for a period of infancy when he had known, if only briefly, his mother's love. He is lying on a hospital bed, cared for by attentive sisters who are responsive to his every need. The memory restores a deeply buried past. Harsh and controlling figure that she was, Vitalie Cuif

Rimbaud did not leave only that negative impression on her son's character. There was some trace of tenderness, some suppressed memory of infancy that surfaces momentarily, although Arthur himself is not fully aware of it. Here is the true "Éclair," the lightning flash out of his past, an expression of love that he can never avow. In fact he *disavows* it, by identifying with the revolutionary Ruel, who smashed the vase containing the "aromates sacrés / sacred ointments," used in the consecration of French kings at Saint-Denis. Ruel hanged himself a year later. A few years after *Une Saison en enfer* was published (in August 1873), unconsciously mimicking Ruel, Rimbaud immolated his genius.

For this brief moment ("l'éclair") he is unconsciously reconciled to his mother; he accepts her love, he makes amends (by the detour of a screen memory) for all the years wasted in revolt and disobedience to her: "Alors,—oh! chère pauvre âme, l'éternité serait-elle pas perdue pour nous!" ("Then,—oh! poor dear soul, wouldn't eternity be saved for us!"). This last line is both question (am I condemned?) and assertion/denial (I am/am not condemned). Rimbaud keeps all his options open.

"Matin"

"Matin" echoes "Jadis" at the beginning of the *Saison,* where life was a "festin où s'ouvraient tous les coeurs, où tous les vins coulaient." Here he writes: "N'eus-je pas *une fois* une jeunesse aimable, héroïque, fabuleuse, à écrire sur des feuilles d'or—trop de chance! / Did I not once have a lovely youth, heroic, fabulous, to be written on leaves of gold—too much luck!" Those first years of happiness are the one thing he knows for sure, the one thing he can wager on. And by the way, Pascal is present throughout *Une Saison.* He is one of Rimbaud's interlocutors and one of his judges. Time and again, the poet seems to wager, now for eternity, now against it. While we began with *Les Fleurs du mal* as the principal intertext for *Une Saison en enfer,* it becomes clear, as the work evolves, that Rimbaud wields with increasing skill a kind of Pascalian ratiocination.

WHAT THEN accounts for his present misery? "Par quel crime, par quelle erreur, ai-je mérité ma faiblesse actuelle? / By what crime, by what error, have I merited my present weakness?" Here sublimation is drawn thin, as Rimbaud opens his heart to the jury in this act of summation. He says in effect: "You who pity slaughtered animals and dying men, explain my fall and my sleep. I can't explain it any more than the beggar with his continual *Our Fathers* and *Hail Marys*." "*Je ne sais plus parler.* / I have forgotten how to speak."

And on this confession he ends: "Pourtant, aujourd'hui, je crois avoir fini la relation de mon enfer. C'était bien l'enfer; l'ancien, celui dont le fils de l'homme ouvrit les portes / Yet today, I've finished the account of my hell. It was really hell; the ancient one, the one whose gates were opened by the son of man." Then comes an evocation of the three wise men, who followed the star of Bethlehem, seen as allegories of heart, soul, mind. He asks:

> Quand irons-nous, par delà les grèves et les monts, saluer la naissance du travail nouveau, la sagesse nouvelle, la fuite des tyrans et des démons, la fin de la superstition, adorer—les premiers!—Noël sur la terre!

> When shall we go, beyond the shores and the mountains, to salute the birth of the new work, the new wisdom, the flight of tyrants and demons, the end of superstition, and be the first to worship Christmas on earth!

With this transliteration of the Nativity Gospel, Rimbaud sublimates his hatred of the Catholic Church. He allegorizes Christianity. We are all beggars who cry out for redemption, "Christmas on earth!" I was in hell, the same hell that Christ harrowed. Now I wait for my rebirth. I await: "Le chant des cieux, la marche des peuples! Esclaves, ne maudissons pas la vie." ("Heaven's song, the marching of peoples! Slaves, let us not curse life!").

Here again we have the crossing of terms: Christmas versus the cursing of life, which equals hell on earth. Waiting, working, watching; all this keeps the argument in suspense, yet emphasizes an *affirmation* of life by use of a negative ("Slaves, let us not curse life!"). Is this a sign of failure, to have come so far, through a forest of dialectic, only to arrive at this negative affirmation? I think not; and one has to admire the poetic and ratiocinative genius that can pose his personal enigma within the centuries-old enigma of Christianity.

We understand why Paul Claudel took Rimbaud as model for his spirituality. Here, as he establishes a final order among his memories of past events and future anticipations, Rimbaud squarely faces his own abjection and, like Job on his bed of pain, refuses to curse his hard lot. Instead, he celebrates it in some of the most memorable poetry ever written. He will continue on through the high desert solitude of Abyssinia, still searching for that horizon Heidegger speaks of. In a certain sense Rimbaud rose from his fallen state to become a new man. Here Rimbaud parts company with Baudelaire, who posited the fallen nature of humankind as the chief tenet of his theology. Considering this courageous reversal of perspective, Claudel wrote of *Une Saison en enfer* that it was "tout entière pénétrée par l'âme / entirely penetrated by soul."[15]

"Matin" is a final masterstroke of sublimation/transformation. By the psychic medicine of poetry, Rimbaud has exorcised his demons—his infantile sexual drives, his bitterness toward Verlaine, his rage against his mother and her church. He has renewed himself and is prepared to face the hostility of Paris and whatever hard luck the future holds. Now, at last, he can affirm life instead of cursing it. This is sublimation in the most positive meaning of the term. He has achieved A'—faith in his own deepest self. This is possible because he has recognized all that is negative, selfish, grasping. It is possible now to accept his own life experience, what he was, what he is, what he will become. He comes very close to the "ego-ideal" that he will celebrate a year or two later in "Génie."

Yet is it necessary to say that—no matter how much he sublimates—he can never be the conventional "bon bourgeois"? Everything that is best in his writing subverts that cliché. From "Le Bateau ivre" to "Aube," from "Barbare" to "Nocturne vulgaire," it is the breakthrough from fantasy to primary process that accounts for the stunning brilliance and mystery of his poems.

"L'automne déjà!"

"L'automne déjà! / Autumn already!"—So begins "Adieu," the last section, recalling, by its adverb of temporality, "Jadis" at the start of the poem. He is resolute, his face turned toward "la clarté divine / the divine light" and the task ahead. The future is London, "la cité énorme au ciel taché de feu et de boue / the enormous city its sky stained by fire and mud." He joins in spirit with the ordinary people of this teeming city: "Ah! les haillons pourris, le pain trempé de pluie, l'ivresse, les mille amours qui m'ont crucifié! / Ah! the rotten rags, the rain-soaked bread, the drunkenness, the thousand loves that have crucified me!" He sees himself as he was, penniless, sick, alone:

> Je me revois la peau rongée par la boue et la peste, des vers plein les cheveux et les aisselles et encore de plus gros vers dans le coeur, étendu

parmi les inconnus sans âge, sans sentiment. . . . J'aurais pu y mourir. . .
L'affreuse évocation! J'exècre la misère.

I see myself skin pitted by mud and pestilence, worms in my hair and armpits and still bigger worms in my heart, stretched out among strangers without age, without feeling . . . I might have died there . . . Horrible thought! I detest poverty.

But he must be on guard against bourgeois temptations: "Et je redoute l'hiver parce que c'est la saison du comfort! / And I dread winter because it's the season of comfort!"[16]

Then comes a sustained passage in which he effortlessly summarizes all his visions, all his magnificent creations—everything that he must renounce:

—Quelquefois je vois au ciel des plages sans fin couvertes de blanches nations en joie. Un grand vaisseau d'or, au-dessus de moi, agite ses pavillons multicolores sous les brises du matin.

—Sometimes I see in the sky endless beaches covered with joyful white nations. A great golden ship, up above me, waves its multicolored pennants in the morning breezes.

This nautical image is not the drunken boat of "Bateau ivre," but the triumphant vessel of his *oeuvre*, his poetic works moving triumphantly into the future:

J'ai créé toutes les fêtes, tous les triomphes, tous les drames. J'ai essayé d'inventer de nouvelles fleurs, de nouveaux astres, de nouvelles chairs, de nouvelles langues. J'ai cru acquérir des pouvoirs surnaturels. Eh bien! je dois enterrer mon imagination et mes souvenirs! Une belle gloire d'artiste et de conteur emportée!

I have created all festivals, all triumphs, all dramas. I tried to invent new flowers, new stars, and flesh, new speech. I believed I had acquired supernatural powers. Well then! I have to bury my imagination and my memories! A great glory as an artist and storyteller swept away!

Now, in a return to his roots, he dismisses *Voyance* and other forms of grandiosity; he realizes that the cost of poetry (his kind of poetry) is too great; it requires withdrawal from the world. He resolves:

Moi! moi qui me suis dit mage ou ange, dispensé de toute morale, je suis rendu au sol, avec un devoir à chercher, et la réalité rugueuse à étreindre! Paysan!

I! I who called myself shaman or angel, exempt from all morality, I'm restored to the earth, with a duty to seek, and rugged reality to embrace! Peasant!

Briefly he looks back with regret:

Suis-je trompé? la charité serait-elle soeur de la mort pour moi? Enfin, je demanderai pardon pour m'être nourri de mensonge. Et allons.
   Mais pas une main amie! et où puiser le secours?

Am I mistaken? would charity be the sister of death for me? Anyway, I'll beg pardon for having subsisted on lies. Now let's go.
   But not one friendly hand! and where find help?

What exactly did he mean by "charity"? The Church defines "charity" as love of God and other human beings—but no matter. He told himself lies about that and many other matters that he resolutely sets behind him. Here, in asking forgiveness, he explicitly makes reparation for nourishing himself with lies.

The hour (of judgment? of action?) that he faces now is harsh, but the sounds of hell ("grincements de dents, sifflements de feu / grinding of teeth, whistling of fire") abate. Even his disgusting memories grow dim. And no more regrets! "Il faut être absolument moderne. / We must be absolutely modern." (Live in the present, face whatever comes down the pike: "tenir le pas gagné ... / keep holding the advantage ... "): "Le combat spirituel est aussi brutal que la bataille d'hommes; mais la vision de la justice est le plaisir de Dieu seul" ("Spiritual war is as brutal as human combat; but the vision of justice is God's pleasure alone").

Rimbaud elides many steps in the argument as he pushes toward his conclusion. The secret of chiasmus is that the outer terms contain and restrain the inner terms that, so to speak, "dwell" within them. This explains the psychic wholeness attained at the end of *Une Saison,* where he asks for "une ardente patience / a *burning* patience" in order to go forth and confront the "splendides villes / the splendid cities." As Heidegger says: "The poetic is the basic capacity for human dwelling.... Man dwells in that he builds ... " (*Poetry, Language, Thought* 226, 225).

Rimbaud concludes, "il me sera loisible de posséder la vérité dans une âme et un corps / I will be allowed to possess truth in one soul and one body." Writing the *Saison* in the isolation of the farmhouse in Roche, he invests his "burning patience" in the creation of a work that will allow him, at this critical juncture in his life, to possess the truth of who and what he is. Armed with this knowledge, he can return to the teeming cities that draw him into the magnetic field of their myriad lives.

After the release of this spiritual battle, where he has exorcised the demon, sublimated his terror and aggression, affirmed his belief in mankind, he opens his heart to tenderness and his body to the surge of vigor that he feels as he marches toward the splendid cities of his future. Alone, no friendly hand, scornful of the delusive passions of "ces couples menteurs . . . / these lying couples . . . ," he affirms:—et il me sera loisible de *posséder la vérité dans une âme et un corps /* —and I shall be allowed *to possess truth in one soul and one body."* The achievement of *Une Saison en enfer* is this act of self-acceptance. Finished the war between mind and the senses, finished those tormented doubts about the validity of love as he has known it. Finished self-hatred and self-disgust. Finished by the trope of chiasmus, where the positive includes and subdues its negation.

Rimbaud has been forced by events to lie, to deceive, to repress or disguise his passions, but all that is past. Truth is somewhere in the future but now, as a whole man, without compromise or anxiety, integrated and free, he can find that truth; he will know it when he perceives it, and, whatever it is, he will make it his own. To paraphrase the last sentence of Hans Loewald's book: *Sublimation is both a mourning of lost original oneness and a celebration of oneness regained.*[17]

Appendix

The Death of Rimbaud

"We remember him and he travels on."

> ... la Vampire qui nous rend gentils
> (... the Vampire who makes us be nice)
>
> —"Angoisse"

In July of 1949 I stood on the Place Jean-Jaurès in Marseilles under a blazing sun and stared up at the yellow walls of the Hôpital de la Conception, where Arthur Rimbaud died on November 10, 1891.[1] He was thirty-seven years old, afflicted with cancer that had eaten into his right knee and metastasized through his body. Amputation of the leg came too late to save him. I remember the heat, the vertigo brought on by two days of travel, and a sense of awe realizing this was the place that the poet I first encountered two years earlier in a University of Chicago classroom had died. It was a three-story building with a central courtyard. There was a dry, metallic taste in the back of my throat. Earlier that spring, I had accompanied my teacher, Wallace Fowlie, to Charleville-Mézières in the Ardennes. We saw Rimbaud's statue, the Collège de Charleville, the Meuse River where he and his brother used to daydream on an old rowboat anchored in the mud. In the hotel w.c. some transient G.I. (perhaps in retreat from the Battle of the Bulge) had scrawled "Kilroy was here."

Fowlie told me details of Rimbaud's two hospitalizations in Marseilles. He first arrived in Marseilles on May 21, 1891:

> Je suis arrivé hier, après treize jours de douleurs. Me trouvant par trop faible à l'arrivée ici, et saisi par le froid, j'ai dû entrer ici à *l'hôpital de la Conception,* où je paie dix francs par jour, docteur compris.
>   Je suis très mal, très mal, je suis réduit à l'état de squelette par cette maladie de ma jambe gauche [should read "droite"] qui est devenue à présent énorme et ressemble à une énorme citrouille. C'est une synovite, une hydarthrose, etc., une maladie des articulations et des os.[2] (Pléiade, 665)

I arrived here yesterday, after thirteen days of pain. Since I was very weak on arriving, and racked by the cold, I had to register here at the *Conception Hospital*, where I pay ten francs a day, doctor included.

I'm sick, very sick, reduced to a skeleton by this disease of my left [should read right] leg which has become enormous and looks like a giant pumpkin. It's a synovitis, a hydarthrose, etc., an inflammation of the joints and the bones.

His mother came from Roche at the time of the amputation, then left again quickly despite all his pleading. Instead Isabelle, his sister, thirty-one years old, came to be with him. Still fighting his immobility, Rimbaud insisted on returning to Roche. The trip up on July 23, 1891, the brief sojourn, then the return trip a month later, was a nightmare. He again checked into the hospital, this time under the name "Jean" Rimbaud.[3] And the agony began.

The days were hellish, he cursed the nuns and orderlies, drove out the hospital chaplains who came by twos. He fought the pain and the proximity of death tormented him. This was the traveler who had written his mother, only a year earlier: "D'ailleurs, il y a une chose qui m'est impossible, c'est la vie sédentaire / Anyway, there is one thing impossible for me, that's a sedentary life" (Pléiade, 641). He was now glued to his hospital bed, reduced to total dependency on his sister. He existed with the unremitting terror that she would desert him, as his mother had done. Isabelle wrote her mother:

> ... quand il dort le jour, il est réveillé en sursaut, il me dit que c'est un coup qui le frappe au coeur et à la tête tout à la fois qui le réveille ainsi; quand il dort la nuit, il a des rêves effrayants et quelquefois quand il se réveille il est raide au point de ne plus pouvoir faire un mouvement, le veilleur de nuit l'a déjà trouvé en cet état, et il sue, il sue jour et nuit par le froid comme par la chaleur. Depuis que la raison lui est revenue il pleure toujours, il ne croit pas encore qu'il restera paralysé (si toutefois il vit). Trompé par les médecins il se cramponne à la vie, à l'espoir de guérir, et comme il se sent toujours bien malade et que maintenant il se rend compte de son état la plupart du temps, il se met à douter de ce qui lui disent les docteurs, il les accuse de se moquer de lui, ou bien il les taxe d'ignorance. (Pléiade 699) [22 Sept., 1891]

> ... when he sleeps during the day, he wakes with a start, he tells me it's like a blow that strikes him in the heart and the head both at once that wakes him; when he sleeps at night, he has terrifying dreams and sometimes when he wakes up he is too stiff to make the slightest movement, the night guard has often found him in that state, and he sweats, he sweats day and night whether it's cold or hot. Since becoming rational he cries constantly, he isn't yet ready to believe that he will be paralyzed (if he lives). Deceived by the doctors, he hangs onto life, to the hope of a cure, and since he still feels very sick and since he is aware of his condition most of the time, he has begun to disbelieve what the doctors tell him, he accuses them of mocking him, or he considers them ignorant.

On October 4 Isabelle writes that when he wakes in the morning:

Il se met alors à me raconter des choses invraisemblables qu'il s'imagine s'être passées à l'hôpital pendant la nuit; c'est la seule réminiscence de délire qui lui reste, mais opiniâtre au point que, tous les matins et plusieurs fois pendant la journée, il me raconte la même absurdité en se fâchant de ce que je n'y croie pas. Je l'écoute donc et cherche à le dissuader; il accuse les infirmiers et même les soeurs de choses abominables et qui ne peuvent exister . . . (Pléiade, 703)

He begins to tell me incredible things that he imagines to have happened in the hospital during the night; it's the only vestige of delirium that remains, but he's stubborn to the point where, every morning and several times during the day, he tells me the same absurdity and gets angry because I don't believe him. So I listen to him and try to talk him out of it; he accuses the nurses and even the sisters of abominable things that can't possibly happen . . . [4]

Then comes the "miracle" of Rimbaud's change of heart. After having twice refused the hospital chaplains, on Sunday, October 25, Rimbaud agrees to receive the Sacrament of Confession. There are three versions of the letter in which Isabelle announced the "miracle" to her mother. Jean-Jacques Lefrère, who gives the three versions in his compendium of Rimbaud's correspondence,[5] concludes that the original, written on October 28, 1891, no longer exists. Instead, the letters that bear witness to Rimbaud's "conversion" are a patchwork, composed by Isabelle ten years after her brother's death, when she was being courted by Paterne Berrichon, who foresaw a chance for fame and fortune in the dead poet's estate.

Claudel and perhaps Mauriac were the only major authors who accepted Isabelle's account of her brother's conversion. The rest denied and continue to deny that the nearly lifelong atheist, who wrote "Les Premières Communions," "Un Coeur sous une soutane / A heart beneath a soutane," "Nos fesses ne sont pas les leurs / Our buns are not like theirs" could have died "le chapelet aux pinces / the rosary between his fingers." The truth of this mystery will never be known.

THE FOLLOWING narration is based on a suggestion by Lefrère that perhaps Rimbaud made his confession to please Isabelle, who spent her days by his hospital bed, terrified of his rages and delusions, unable to sleep at night, sustained by her religious faith and her devotion to Arthur. It was the one thing he could do to please her, the one expedient that might persuade her to stay. She writes her mother on Wednesday, October 28:

Dimanche matin, après la grand-messe, il semblait plus calme et en pleine connaissance: l'un des aumoniers est revenu et lui a proposé de se confesser; et il a bien voulu! Quand le prêtre est sorti, il m'a dit, en me regardant d'un air troublé, d'un air étrange: "Votre frère a la foi, mon enfant, que nous disiez-vous donc? Il a la foi, et je n'ai même jamais vu de foi de cette qualité!"
[. . .]
   Quand je suis rentrée près de lui, il était très ému, mais ne pleurait pas; il était sereinement triste, comme je ne l'ai jamais vu. Il me regardait dans les yeux

comme il ne m'a jamais regardée. Il a voulu que j'approche tout près, il m'a dit: "Tu es du même sang que moi: crois-tu, dis, crois-tu?" J'ai répondu: "Je crois; d'autres bien plus savants que moi ont cru, croient; et puis je suis sûre à présent, j'ai la preuve, cela est!" ... Il m'a dit encore avec amertume: "Oui, ils disent qu'ils croient, ils font semblant d'être convertis, mais c'est pour qu'on lise ce qu'ils écrivent, c'est une spéculation!" (Pléiade, 704–5)

Sunday morning, after the high mass, he seemed calm and fully aware: one of the chaplains came and offered to hear his confession; and he agreed! When the priest left, he told me, "Your brother has faith, my child, what were you telling us? He has faith and I have never before seen faith of that quality!"
[...]
When I came back to be with him, he was very moved, but he wasn't crying; he was serenely sad, in a way I've never seen him before. He looked me in the eyes in a way he's never done before. He wanted me close to him, he said, "You are of the same blood as I am: do you believe?" I replied: "I believe; others, much wiser than I am have believed, do believe; and now I'm certain, I have the proof, once and for all!" And it's true, I have the proof today!–He said to me with bitterness: "Yes, they say they believe, they pretend to be converted, but it's so that people will read what they write, it's a speculation!"

Isabelle has been accused of lying and downright fabrication. Nicholl, less crudely, thinks she "dreamed" Rimbaud's conversion during her own troubled nights. I believe that the original letter was doctored up but that the Confession actually took place. There is this evidence: First, she would not commit the gratuitous sin of lying to her mother about something both held sacred. Second (and in Lefrère's opinion) the most convincing indication is the following: "One single element—but weighty—points to a judgment of authenticity: the final paragraph, in which Isabelle explains to her mother that she should not count on receiving any money from her son after his death: these lines appear so hard for the mother that they lend a stamp of authenticity to those that precede ... " (952). Third, the priest's words have the ring of professionalism. It's hard to believe that Isabelle invented them. Fourth, Arthur's statements about profiting from a "false conversion," with its recollection of Verlaine and *Une Saison en enfer,* also have the stamp of authenticity. And fifth, venality, as evoked, for instance, in "Le Mal," was always a sin that Rimbaud associated with the Church. Why would Isabelle invent these things that are so frankly embarrassing for her faith? Writing only a few days after the event, I think Isabelle gives an honest picture of what happened in Arthur's sickroom in La Conception. Besides, hadn't he predicted it when he wrote "Angoisse" and evoked "La Vampire qui nous rend gentils"? The proximity of death brings unexpected changes—even Voltaire died with priests and candles. As in so many other respects, Rimbaud was prescient about his end.

If he began the confession as a gift to his sister, he must have been caught up in this unique opportunity to review his life and see how it added up in the perspective of traditional values: did he amount to something—or was his life a zero-sum game?

LATER, WITH THE connivance of her future husband, the grotesque Paterne Berrichon,[6] Isabelle tried to reinvent her brother. Yves Reboul is the sharpest critic of Isabelle Rimbaud: "After her myth about *Voyance,* that other traditional rimbaldian problem, there is the meaning of the *Illuminations,* another problem that owes its existence and most especially the way it is posed to the lies and the legends spread in profusion by Rimbaud's sister."[7] She painted him as a shaman or a saint; Claudel's more guarded epithet, "a mystic in a savage state," has the echo of Isabelle's influence. She will try, with small success, to fashion this myth after his death.

But it was not just her misguided desire to protect the family that led her astray. The discovery of his work, especially the *Illuminations,* infected her with the poetry virus. Surely she too had inherited some of Arthur's magical powers. This must be the way she justified to herself changing his words, which should have otherwise been sacred.

His suffering, witnessed for weeks on end, commanded her belief in him. Although, as death approached, he lost lucidity more and more frequently, he had a secret magnetism, an authority that caused the priest to comment, "I have never before heard a confession of that quality." This is a professional man, a hospital chaplain, who often ministered to the dying. Almost grudgingly, he bestows his accolade: "une confession de cette qualité." Chaulier was astonished by the intensity of this penitent, moved by his passion for life even as it slipped away in each labored breath.

We can't help wondering what Rimbaud, thirty-seven years old and dying with the atrocious pain of his malignancy, can have confessed or how he confessed. In short, hammered phrases, broken by ironic gasps that turn to sobs. Looking into the past, beyond the priest, who sits by his bedside, he first recognizes the canonical sins defined by Catholic morality: acts of dishonesty, deception, lies (yes, there were plenty of those). Then anger, especially at his mother, a woman of limited intelligence who never understood her son. And his "vice," his sexual preference, to use the euphemism we prefer today. This is something the priest knows at first hand. He has spent years in seminaries; he understands the variety of carnal appetites. But there is something else. This man, with the thin dark face, the cavernous eyes, the graying hair, this young man gripping the sheets, nailed to the bed beside him has a secret. It is a secret that devours him, that won't let him die peacefully or accept this terrible outcome as his burden, his path to follow out of this world. We can only wonder about that secret; but I think it is what Baudelaire expresses in "La servante au grand coeur . . . / the great-hearted servant . . . " where he writes:

> Si, par une nuit bleue et froide de décembre,
> Je la trouvais tapie en un coin de ma chambre,
> Grave, et venant du fond de son lit éternel
> Couver l'enfant grandi de son oeil maternel,
> Que pourrais-je répondre a cette âme pieuse,
> Voyant tomber des pleurs de sa paupière creuse?
>
> If, one blue and cold December night,
> I found her crouched in a corner of my room,

Solemn, come from her eternal bed
To nurse the child grown under her maternal gaze,
What could I reply to that pious soul,
Watching tears fall from her hollow eyes?[8]

Rimbaud—like Baudelaire—remembers someone who looks at him with mingled love and compassion, someone who asks wordlessly: "What have you done with your life? with your genius? with all the promise of youth?" It is neither his mother nor his sister, neither Izambard nor Verlaine. This questioner is his own *Génie*. It is what he expects from himself, what he has dreamed of, aspired toward. The ego-ideal, though born in the unconscious, is considered by Freud as the representative of reality and serves as a "reference point for the ego's evaluation of its real achievements" (Laplanche, 144). Even more important than this retrospective function, the ego-ideal defines the goals toward which the individual strives and in terms of which he will make his self-evaluation. Bitterly, Rimbaud concedes that he hasn't lived up to that standard:

O Lui et nous! l'orgueil plus bienveillant que les charités perdues.
O monde! et le chant clair des malheurs nouveaux!
Il nous a connus tous et nous a tous aimés. Sachons, cette nuit d'hiver, de cap en cap, du pôle tumultueux au château, de la foule à la plage, de regards en regards, forces et sentiments las, le héler et le voir, et le renvoyer, et sous les marées et au haut des déserts de neige, suivre ses vues, ses souffles, son corps, son jour.

O he and us! pride more benevolent than all lost charities.
O world! and clear song of new misfortunes!
He has known us all and has loved us all. May we know, this winter's night, from cape to cape, from tumultuous pole to the chateau, from the crowd to the beach, from glance to glance, weary in sentiment and strength, to hail him and see him, and send him on, and under the tides and above the deserts of snow, follow his visions, his breaths, his body, his day.

Can the priest sense what this man will give to generations not yet born? Does he recognize the possibility of misjudgment in Rimbaud's *examen de conscience?* Chaulier is transfixed by a voice that whispers from a burning heart, carefully aligning its mistakes and failures.

Rimbaud brushes aside the priest's consolation. He has been brave in the face of danger, he has slaved at bitter tasks in the matted African bush. He has saved gold thalers in a money belt. But, in some deeper, more fundamental sense, he has failed. He tells the priest that he has wasted his life, wasted his gifts, thrown them away on illusions. And he wonders if even this confession is not another illusion.

THIS IS THE ultimate price Rimbaud paid for genius—to believe he had wasted it, thrown it away. Canon Chaulier gives the dying man absolution and a penance of one Our Father and one Hail Mary. Then he anoints him. It is impossible to return with the Eucharist. Rimbaud cannot hold anything down. He is ready for the journey anticipated in "Le Bateau ivre"—"O que ma quille éclate / O que j'aille à la mer! / O may my keel break / O may I go to the sea!"

RETURNING FOR a moment to Isabelle, it is important to record that she was the tutelary spirit (as the Africans see the ancestral being who accompanies a dying person) or, in the Buddhist tradition, the bodhisattva, who performs the same role.[9] That was why he asked her: "Do you believe? We are of the same blood! Do you believe, tell me, do you believe?"

Rimbaud took heart from Isabelle's faith because the source of deep religious belief is not in sacred writings but, more often than not, in the devotion of the companion spirit who delivers us to death's door.

In his last delirium before death, on November 9, 1891, he dictates a letter to Isabelle. It is addressed to the director of the Messageries Maritimes steamship company in Marseilles. It reads:

ONE LOT: A SINGLE TUSK
ONE LOT: TWO TUSKS
ONE LOT: THREE TUSKS
ONE LOT: FOUR TUSKS
ONE LOT: TWO TUSKS
[Note: The list of elephant ivory was on the already used paper when Isabelle began to write.]
Dear Sir:
I have come to enquire if I have anything left on account with you. I wish to change today my booking on this ship whose name I don't even know, but anyway it must be the ship from Aphinar. There are shipping lines going all over the place, but helpless and unhappy as I am, I can't find a single one—the first dog you meet on the street will tell you this. Send me the prices of the ship from Aphinar to Suez. I am completely paralyzed, so I wish to embark in good time. Please let me know when I should be carried aboard . . . [10]

Charles Nicholl comments:

Where or what Aphinar is no one is sure. The phrase he uses is "le service d'Aphinar," which seems to mean "the ship from Aphinar" but could equally mean "the Aphinar shipping line," so one cannot be quite sure if Aphinar is a place or a company, or even a particular captain. One cannot even be sure that "Aphinar" is what Rimbaud said: it is only Isabelle's transcription. Was it rather Al Finar, the Arab word for "lighthouse," and was this the phantom ship which he wished to board "in good time" the one that would carry him away from light and into darkness? (310–11)

Or perhaps from darkness into the light? He died thirteen hours later on November 10, 1891. His former employer, Alfred Bardey, was one of the many who paid tribute to him (eulogized is too strong a word): "He was one of the first pioneers at Harar, and all who have known him over the last eleven years will tell you that he was an honest, capable and courageous man" (Nicholl, 313).

To answer Heidegger's question posed in the epigraph to this book, we can say that the poetry gives us clues to the horizons of Rimbaud's inner life, but what he found on the other shore remains beyond interpretation.

Notes

Introduction

1. J.-L. Baudry, "Le Texte de Rimbaud," *Tel Quel* 35 and 36 (46).
2. Suzanne Briet, *Madame Rimbaud/essai de biographie,* 72.
3. Jean-Pierre Richard is an exception here, since he finds no depth in Rimbaud, only a dazzling surface: "Rimbaud rejects all manifestations of depth, and it is this which marks his real divorce from Baudelaire. His visions display themselves on a shallow screen; film-strips supremely thin and yet unbreakable for there is nothing behind them, neither volume nor abyss nor being nor nothingness nor god nor the infinite. . . ." *Poésie et profondeur,* 240. But Richard is speaking of the iconic image-work here, not the subjective depth of poetic consciousness.
4. The recent book by Todd Dufresne, *Against Freud: Critics Talk Back,* gives some idea of the contradictions, confusions, and errors attributed to Freudianism by a mixed bag of critics. Because of the interview format, this book is a collection of opinions rather than closely argued positions.
5. Charles Guignon, ed. *The Cambridge Companion to Heidegger,* 25.
6. On the uncanny see David Ellison, *Ethics and Aesthetics in European Modernist Literature: From the Sublime to the Uncanny.* Ellison gives a striking analysis of Freud's unconscious motivation in writing "Das Unheimliche" ("The Uncanny"): "If, to use Freud's own vocabulary, one might say that the conscious purpose of his essay 'Das Unheimliche' was to remove the uncanny from the domain of the aesthetic and reterritorialize it within the field of psychoanalytic theory, its unconscious motivation would seem to be the instantiation of the repetition compulsion in a literary model" (67).
7. The concept of "the splitting of the ego" in respect to perceived reality

originates with Janet, Breuer, and Freud; here, I have taken my theoretical reference from Melanie Klein's reworking of the original thesis.

8. Marjorie Perloff, *The Poetics of Indeterminacy: Rimbaud to Cage*. I am using the edition republished by Northwestern University Press, 1983.

9. This was the priest who signed the death certificate. He was sixty years old in 1891. There was another, much younger priest at the hospital, but the comments reported by Isabelle are those of an older man.

10. André Guyaux, *Poétique du Fragment, essai; Illuminations, Texte établi et commenté par A.G.*

Chapter 1

1. Elizabeth Wright, *Psychoanalytic Criticism: Theory in Practice*, 1.
2. C. A. Hackett, *Rimbaud l'Enfant*.
3. Charles Baudelaire, "Le Génie enfant," in *Oeuvres*, vol. I: 380.
4. Yves Bonnefoy, *Rimbaud*, 2nd ed., 1994.
5. Leo Bersani, *A Future for Astyanax: Character and Desire in Literature*, 254.
6. George Steiner, *Real Presences*, 99.
7. Graham Robb, *Rimbaud*.
8. Pierre Brunel, *Arthur Rimbaud ou l'éclatant désastre*.
9. Leo Bersani, *The Culture of Redemption*.
10. This might be compared to Lacan's view that the psyche is structured like a text or Derrida's inverse position, that the text has features of the psyche, e.g., it is a weave of memory "traces."
11. Michel Collot, *L'Horizon fabuleux*, Vol. 1, *XIXe siècle*.
12. The concept of *dwelling* is taken from a prose poem by Hölderlin ("In Lieblicher Bläue . . . / In Lovely Blueness"), who writes, "Full of acquirements, but poetically man dwells on this earth." Friedrich Hölderlin, *Poems and Fragments*, trans. Michael Hamburger (Ann Arbor: The University of Michigan Press, 1967), 600–1. Heidegger unpacks this seemingly simple phrase, first separating poetic existence from the busyness of modern life, and then giving it the attribute of an essential humanity that comes to us in the appeal of language. So it is that man/woman dwells and has his/her being in "the house of language."
13. Sergio Sacchi, *Etudes sur les* Illuminations *de Rimbaud*.
14. "Exercice de mémoire," *Revue de l'Université de Bruxelles* 1–2 (1982): 47–60.
15. Jean-Luc Steinmetz, "Ici, Maintenant, Les *Illuminations*," *Littérature* (1972): 22–45.
16. Hans W. Loewald, M.D., *Sublimation: Inquiries into Theoretical Psychoanalysis*.
17. Formulae such as "Oedipus complex" or "primal scene" are part concept and part image, which allows them to be used simultaneously as figures and analytical terms.
18. Lanham, Richard A. *A Handlist of Rhetorical Terms*, 99.
19. In his essay on Rimbaud, Collot illustrates the figural nature of psychocritical language, as for instance in the following: "Dans le jeu des figures qui trament

son écriture, c'est *le je* qui est mis en jeu, et son histoire qui prend figure. / In the play of figures which frames his writing, it is the *I* that is put in play, and its story that is figured" (160).

Chapter 2

1. "La Bouche d'ombre" is a weighty metaphysical poem by Victor Hugo.
2. Enid Starkie believed that Rimbaud had read books on alchemy and magic in the Charleville library. He certainly studied Michelet's *La Sorcière* and Quinet's *Le Génie des Religions*. Starkie finds evidence for familiarity with alchemy in his sonnet "Voyelles." (There are many sources for this poem, but the most obvious is Baudelaire's "Correspondances.") Starkie comments on other more esoteric writers but there is no clear evidence that Rimbaud read them. Enid Starkie, *Arthur Rimbaud*, 159–78.
3. Herbert L. Dreyfus, "Heidegger on the connection between nihilism, art, technology, and politics," in *The Cambridge Companion to Heidegger*, 293.
4. Lawler, *Rimbaud's Theatre of the Self*, 130.
5. Citations are from the book of essays by Martin Heidegger, *Poetry, Language, Thought*, selected and translated by Albert Hofstadter.

Chapter 3

1. David Ellison writes about Freud's invention of the uncanny as a theorization that is unconsciously literary; this observation supports the point made in chapter 1, about the figurative nature of many psychoanalytic formulae. See Ellison's *Ethics and Aesthetics in European Modernist Literature: From the Sublime to the Uncanny*, 67.
2. Sigmund Freud, *The Uncanny*, trans. David McLintock, 135.
3. Enid Starkie, *Arthur Rimbaud*, 97–98.
4. Jean-Lacques Lefrère, *Arthur Rimbaud*, 311.
5. James Lawler, "The Poet as Transgressor: 'Le Bateau ivre,'" in *Rimbaud's Theatre of the Self*.
6. Paul Verlaine, *Oeuvres en prose complètes*, 753–54.
7. Neil Hertz, "Freud and the Sandman," in *The End of the Line*, 101–2.
8. The Freudian equation of phallus = eyes is based on the relation of both to sexual desire. In "Le Bateau ivre" the menacing eyes may represent the father's phallus, both threat and object of intense infantile curiosity. Taken more literally, the prison scows actually existed at the time Rimbaud wrote his poem. They held the communards who had rebelled against the government.
9. Robert J. Dostal, "Time and phenomenology in Husserl and Heidegger," in *The Cambridge Companion to Heidegger*, 156.

Chapter 4

1. Paul Claudel, "Préface," *Oeuvres d'Arthur Rimbaud*, 13.

2. Atle Kittang, *Discours et jeu: essai d'analyse des textes d'Arthur Rimbaud*, 204.

3. James Lawler, "The Poet as Memorialist," in *Rimbaud's Theatre of the Self*, 54–66.

4. Lawler makes a connection between Mémoire and the draft of *Une Saison en enfer*. Rimbaud's plan (never realized) was to see this exploration of memory as a near-death experience. He writes in the draft of *Saison*: "I found myself ripe for death and my weakness led me to the very boundaries of the world and of life"(Lawler, 57).

5. Ross Chambers, "'Mémoire' de Rimbaud: Essai de Lecture,"in *Essays in French Literature*, vol. 5, 1968: 22–37.

6. A splendid example of "vocalise" is Rachmaninoff's Opus 34.

7. Leo Bersani, *A Future for Astyanax*, 242–43.

8. It can in fact be read as a version of the "negative Oedipus complex" in which the father's departure leaves a dominant mother.

9. For both Freud and Klein, the ego has unconscious as well as conscious dimensions.

10. Collot finds a more positive vestige of the primal scene in "l'ébat des anges / the play of angels" in line five.

11. Suzanne Briet, *Madame Rimbaud: essai de biographie*, 13.

12. Blue eyes, he tells us in "Les Poètes de sept ans," are eyes that lie. His own blue eyes had been called "shifty" by Verlaine's wife after her first meeting with Rimbaud. The association of yellow with marriage suggests the taint of cuckoldry.

13. J. Laplanche and J. B. Pontalis, *The Language of Psycho-Analysis*, trans. Donald Nicholson-Smith, 259.

14. Charles W. Socarides, M.D., *The Overt Homosexual*, 23.

Chapter 5

1. The second mystery, which is discussed in the appendix, concerns Rimbaud's deathbed confession. The only evidence for this is a letter from his sister, Isabelle, a less than trustworthy witness.

2. Jean-Jacques Lefrère, *Arthur Rimbaud*, 252.

3. Edward S. Mason, *The Paris Commune*, 116–17.

4. The triolet is a fixed form, made up of eight lines. The first line repeats after the third, the first two after the sixth.

5. This extensively revised poem has had three titles: "Tortured Heart," "Clown's Heart," and "Stolen Heart." I use Verlaine's copy, the one chosen by Suzanne Bernard in her edition.

6. "Ils font des fresques / they make frescoes" is sometimes read by translators to mean obscene graffiti; but to anyone who has experienced barracks life, the pantomime of sexual acts is more plausible. No soldier would incur the sergeant's wrath by defacing the barracks walls.

7. D. W. Winnicott, "On the Use of an Object," in *Psycho-analytic Explorations*, 245–46.

8. Charles D. Minahen, "Tourbillons de lumière," *Stanford French Review* (Winter 1985): 351–64. Minahen also finds this vortical movement in the *Illuminations* "Marine," "Mouvement," and "Mystique." His analysis undercuts the view of J. P. Richard that Rimbaud's iconography is wholly one of surfaces.

9. Charles D. Minahen, *Vortex/t: the Poetics of Turbulence*.

Chapter 6

1. Fourier published *L'Harmonie universelle* in 1804.

2. Jules Michelet, author of *L'Amour / Love* (1858) had two great loves. The first reconciled him to his mother; the second reconciled him to the Orient. In both respects Michelet was important for Rimbaud.

3. There were many indiscriminate killings, though orders were given to kill only activist Communards (especially foreigners), deserters from the army, and men bearing arms.

4. Rimbaud, *Oeuvres*, 257.

5. Kristin Ross, *The Emergence of Social Space: Rimbaud and the Paris Commune*, 152, n1.

Chapter 7

1. Sigmund Freud, "On Narcissism," *The Standard Edition of the Complete Psychological Works*, vol. xiv: 75, trans. James Strachey and Anna Freud.

2. Albert Henry, *Contributions à la lecture de Rimbaud*, 23.

3. Melanie Klein, "The Early Development of Conscience in the Child," in *Love, Guilt and Reparation and Other Works 1921–1945*, vol. 1: 254.

4. This is Klein's response to the unanswerable question about human evil. Marx thought it was man's alienation from his work; Freud blamed the trauma of birth. Rimbaud finds it in a child's boredom.

5. Leo Bersani comments on both the painterly and theatrical framing of the *Illuminations*: "The fabulous atmosphere of Rimbaud's visions is, for example, heightened by Rimbaud's emphasis on their theatrical nature; they are often presented as acts or episodes in some extravagant 'play' of the imagination.... The *Illuminations* should be seen entirely, and at once; our eyes should immediately grasp the entire picture." "Rimbaud's Simplicity," in *A Future for Astyanax*, 252, 253.

6. The "colored plates" may be colored lithographs or the "planches de couleur" from which the lithos are printed. Or possibly the reference is to "enluminures" (as in "illuminated manuscripts").

Chapter 8

1. This group of poets and artists, including Verlaine and Rimbaud, is pictured in the famous painting by Fantin-Latour, "Coin de la Table / Corner of the

Table." Rimbaud attacked a certain Carjat, who threw him out of the meeting for punctuating a poetry recitation with the word "merde." His weapon was a swordcane, and he wounded Carjat in the wrist and the groin.

2. The classical name for abreaction is *catharsis*, that purification/purgation which has both medical and religious connotations. In Aristotle, the homeopathic notion of curing a disorder by inducing that disorder in a controlled way is applied to the symbolic evocation of pity and fear and their unbinding through the tragic action. This is the same process of tension and release clinically described as abreaction.

3. Sigmund Freud, "An Autobiographical Study," in *The Freud Reader*, ed. Peter Gay, 13.

4. Monts-Rocheux is a play on the name of Rimbaud's village, "Roche."

5. Clive Scott, *A Question of Syllables: Essays in Nineteenth-Century French Verse*, x.

6. "Dévotion" is the third poem with an affective title.

7. Arthur Mitzman, *Michelet, Historian*, 195.

8. Rimbaud also uses this device of personification in "Après le déluge" where the flowers gaze wide-eyed at a brand new world.

Chapter 9

1. Another way to read this conclusion is in terms of the pleasure/punishment pairing that is basic to psychoanalysis. Searl speaks of "better than reality" fantasies vs. those that are "worse than reality." They inevitably occur together. (N. Searl, "The Flight to Reality," 280). In such a case the "you" would be Rimbaud himself.

2. The imperial prince, son of Louis-Napoleon, was born in 1856, the year after the International Exposition where Hortense Schneider achieved her greatest success in the role of the Duchess of Gérolstein. He died on June 1, 1879 at the age of twenty-three, killed by Zulu warriors while serving with the British Army in Africa.

3. See my analysis of "Conte" (chapter 10) for a discussion of "monstrous" fantasies.

Chapter 10

1. From the record album by Roberta Flack, *Killing Me Softly* (New York: Atlantic Recording Corp., 1973). The title song is: "Killing Me Softly with His Song."

2. Leo Bersani, "Persons in Pieces," in *A Future for Astyanax*, 290.

3. André Guyaux, *Poétique du fragment*, 205.

4. Lawler attributes the discovery of the relation between Baudelaire's prose poem and "Conte" to Hackett in his edition of the *Oeuvres poétiques* of Rimbaud.

5. Fanciulle is involved in a conspiracy to depose the Prince. Having learned

of the conspiracy, the Prince must inevitably punish the conspirators with death.

6. The *chassé-croisé* is an eighteenth-century dance, where the partners pass alternately in front of and behind each other.

7. These lines from "Délire I: Vierge folle" have the ring of truth:

> Plusieurs nuits, son démon me saisissant, nous nous roulions, je luttais avec lui!—Les nuits, souvent ivre, il se poste dans des rues ou dans des maisons, pour m'épouvanter mortellement.—"On me coupera vraiment le cou; ce sera dégoûtant." Oh! ces jours où il veut marcher avec l'air du crime!

> Several nights, his demon grabbing me, we rolled on the ground, I wrestled with him!—Many nights, often drunk, he hid in the streets or in houses, to scare me to death.—"He'll cut my throat; how disgusting." Oh! those days when he wants to lurk like a criminal!

8. Daniel Lagache, "Situation de l'Aggressivité," *Oeuvres IV,* ed. établie par Eva Rosenblum, 155. Lagache borrows the term "looking-glass self" from the pragmatist Charles H. Cooley.

9. Graham Robb, *Rimbaud.*

Chapter 11

1. Stephen A. Mitchell and Margaret J. Black, *Freud and Beyond: A History of Modern Psychoanalytic Thought,* 87–88.

2. Here I am following the analysis of Laplanche and Pontalis, *The Language of Psycho-analysis,* 298–99.

3. *The Selected Melanie Klein,* ed. Juliet Mitchell, 88.

4. Joseph Pineau, *Le Mouvement rythmique en français,* 13.

Chapter 12

1. Social romanticism was precursor to the humanitarian socialism of Michelet. Arthur Mitzman speaks of Saint-Simonian ideals and values: "A secular religion of humanity, in which artists would take the place of priests, would replace Christianity." *Michelet, Historian,* 13.

2. Sigmund Freud, "The Ego and the Id," in *Complete Psychological Works of Sigmund Freud,* trans. and ed. James Strachey, vol. xix: 37.

3. Freud's view of the relationship between super-ego and ego-ideal shifted between one of independence to one of part to whole.

4. Sigmund Freud, *New Introductory Lectures on Psychoanalysis,* 531.

5. Daniel Lagache, "Structure de la personnalité," *Oeuvres IV,* ed. Eva Rosenblum, 219.

6. Heidegger speaks of the "unshieldedness" of vision, "the innermost of the inner," as opposed to the "presence of calculated objects" in modern metaphysics.

Only with this poet's vision does "the widest orbit of beings become present in the heart's inner space." Martin Heidegger, *Poetry, Language, Thought*, 124–25.

7. François Claudel, "Rimbaud chez Claudel ou une visite à Brangues," *Rimbaud Vivant* 45: 117.

Chapter 13

1. Jim Harrison, *New York Times Book Review*, January 28, 2007.
2. "For Heidegger, the site or essential place of language is the place of a 'gathering into *Ereignis*,' the locus or manifestation . . . to the rift of the Differing, the articulating 'threshold' which intimately conjoins 'world' (here a name for the four-fold mirror play of presencing) and 'things,' while also keeping them strictly parted. . . . This conjoining yet parting threshold is pain, because in its implacable 'stoniness,' it repudiates the human desire for comprehensive unification and grounding." Véronique M. Foti, *Heidegger and the Poets*, 24.
3. These remarks on Heidegger are inspired by *Poetry, Language, Thought*, translated and commented by Albert Hofstadter.
4. This is called "narcissistic ego enrichment" by the *Encyclopedia of Psychoanalysis*, ed. Ludwig Eidelberg, M.D., 327.
5. Otto Fenichel, M.D., *The Psychoanalytic Theory of Neurosis*, 461.
6. Alcohol gave the impetus to Verlaine's madness. Delahaye writes: "Rimbaud me disait de lui: 'Très gentil, mais . . . s'il est ivre, inutile de discuter, parce qu'alors il tire son couteau et on n'a plus qu'à ficher le camp . . . '" ("Rimbaud told me: 'He's very nice, but . . . if he's drunk, it's useless to talk because then he pulls out his knife and all one can do is scram . . . '"). Ernest Delahaye, *Rimbaud: L'Artiste et l'être moral*, 158.
7. Rimbaud uses the English word "comforts" in the original.
8. The spelling "inquestionable" with one "n" rather than two is another anglicism.

Chapter 14

1. Heidegger's reply to an inquiry by R. Munier, "Aujourd'hui Rimbaud," *Archives les Lettres Modernes* N. 160: 12, 14 (emphasis in original)
2. Marjorie Perloff, *The Poetics of Indeterminacy: Rimbaud to Cage*, 66. First published in 1981 by Princeton University Press.
3. Introduction, *The Cambridge Companion to Heidegger*, ed. Charles Guignon, 17.
4. From "la lettre du voyant / the letter of the seer."
5. Charles Taylor, "Heidegger, Language, and Ecology," in *Heidegger: A Critical Reader*, ed. Hubert Dreyfus and Harrison Hall, 256.
6. Martin Heidegger, *Off the Beaten Track*, trans. J. Young and K. Haynes, 51–52, 63.
7. The term is from Dorothea Frede, "The Question of Being," in *The Cambridge Companion to Heidegger*, 46. Heidegger states in *Being and Time* that being

itself is presence; but he also rejects the Aristotelian theory of time as "a manifold of Nows" since time involves a "having been" and an "about to be" and thus contains past and future. Frederick A. Olafson, "The Unity of Heidegger's Thought," in *The Cambridge Companion to Heidegger*, 103.

8. "Madame Rimbaud," trans. Jean Stewart, in *Yves Bonnefoy: The Act and the Place of Poetry, Selected Essays,* ed. John T. Naughton.

9. Roland Barthes, *Le Plaisir du texte,* 17.

10. Raymond J. McCall, *Phenomenological Psychology: An Introduction,* 90.

11. Martin Heidegger, quoted by Charles Taylor, in "Heidegger, Language, and Ecology," 256.

12. On this topic see Hubert L. Dreyfus, "Heidegger's Ontology of Art," in *A Companion to Heidegger,* ed. H. Dreyfus and M. Wrathall (Oxford: Blackwell Publishing Ltd., 2005), 407–19.

Chapter 15

1. He had worked at the Hôtel de Ville during the Commune and fraternized with the communards, but was in no danger.

2. This violence was not something new. When drunk, Verlaine was always prone to violence. He physically abused his wife and on at least four occasions tried to maim or kill his mother.

3. The best proof of Verlaine's influence is Rimbaud's poetry. Of special interest is James Lawler's study of "Dévotion," a poem long considered impenetrable. Lawler shows how Verlaine's name, his persona, his poems are secretly woven into this verbal tapestry. "The Poet as Lover," *Rimbaud's Theatre of the Self,* 191–99.

4. Paul Valéry, *Cahiers,* vol. 29: 871.

5. "The 'nothing' with which anxiety brings us face to face, unveils the nullity by which Dasein [human consciousness], in its very *basis* is defined; and this basis is itself as thrownness into death." Martin Heidegger, *Being and Time,* trans. John Macquarrie and Edward Robinson, 356.

6. The psychoanalytic sources culled in this book are, by and large, based on the naturalism of Freud, which views the subject as "a self-encapsulated center of action" (Guignon, 219). But Rimbaud's own psychology appears free from such a restrictive bias.

7. François Mauriac writes of Baudelaire, "Down to his dying day, he listened to his poor soul and he confessed it. The flowers of evil are the flowers of sin, of repentance, of remorse and penitence." "Charles Baudelaire the Catholic," in *Baudelaire,* ed. Henri Peyre, 30.

8. Natural law (which ruled Rimbaud an outlaw) is synonymous with the substance ontology challenged, undermined, and subverted by Heidegger.

9. Baudelaire's relationship with his mother was complex, but it included a period of mutual affection shortly after the death of his father. The child was six years old. Recalling this at forty he writes, "There was a phase in my childhood of passionate love for you . . . for me that was the blissful time of motherly affection . . . it was probably a bad time for you. But I was always living in you;

you were mine alone, at one and the same time my companion and someone I idolized." From F. W. J. Hemmings, *Baudelaire the Damned: A Biography*, 11.

10. Here again is a Heideggerean theme, the "reassumption" of our heritage that becomes possible once we have discarded the posturing of inauthenticity. See Piotr Hoffman's "Death, time, history: Division II of *Being and Time*," in *The Cambridge Companion to Heidegger*, 212–213.

11. The three surviving sketches are: "A Samarie, plusieurs ont manifesté leur foi en lui/In Samaria, several showed their faith in him"; "L'air léger et charmant de la Galilée" / "The cool and charming air of Galilee"; "Bethsaida, la piscine des cinq galéries / Bethsaida, the pool with five ledges."

12. Some time during the fall of 1872 Rimbaud wrote to his mother, informing her of Verlaine's legal difficulties and his own involvement. Petitfils writes: "Mme Rimbaud received the news as an attack on the honor of her name. Her son involved in a legal case, and suspected of some abominable vice . . . " (162). It seems likely that Mme Rimbaud understood the nature of the relationship between the two poets but refused to admit it.

13. It was Verlaine himself who invented the anagram for his 1886 article in *La Vogue*. As for *Les Poètes maudits* (first ed. 1884), it contained one of his many tributes to Rimbaud, along with eulogies of Corbière, Mallarmé, Villiers de L'Isle-Adam, etc.

14. Heidegger distinguishes between the ordinary guilt of minor omissions and failures and the ontological guilt that arises from Dasein's lack of power over its "thrownness," i.e., the inevitability of death. But the "ordinary guilt" that we experience daily is colored by the awareness of that ultimate "punishment" we know awaits us all.

15. Lawler gives an account of the differing views of the *Saison* held by Valéry and Claudel in his *Rimbaud's Theatre of the Self*, 218.

16. Again, Rimbaud uses the English word "comfort."

17. Loewald asks this as a question: "Could sublimation be both a mourning of lost original oneness and a celebration of oneness regained?" Hans W. Loewald, M.D., *Sublimation: Inquiries into Theoretical Psychoanalysis*, 81.

Appendix

1. The hospital has been rebuilt since I saw it and none of the original "pavillon des malades payants / pavilion of paying patients," where Rimbaud was interned, remains.

2. "Synovitis" is inflammation of the knee joint. It may have been caused by collision with a tree, during a wild horseback ride in Africa. "Hydarthrose" is, according to Charles Nicholl, "an obsolete synonym for arthritis" (286). Nicholl remarks that Rimbaud does not use the word "neoplasm"—meaning cancer—in this, his first letter from the hospital in Marseilles.

3. It is true that his complete name was "Jean-Nicolas-Arthur Rimbaud," but he never used the "Jean-Nicolas." I see this as a sign of the hallucinatory state (attributable to both morphine and pain) in which he lived during the last months of his life.

4. It is ironic that the one poem of Rimbaud's read by many college students is "Le Dormeur du val / Sleeper in the Valley," a pastoral poem based on the sight of a young soldier, lying dead on a battlefield of the Franco-Prussian War. He seems only to sleep, not to have irrevocably crossed the horizon of temporality.

5. Jean-Jacques Lefrère, *Arthur Rimbaud: Correspondance.*

6. Claudel describes Berrichon as follows: "He was an extraordinary fellow, big belly, bald, short, with a beard that hung down to his knees; Berrichon looked like one of those ceramic gnomes that Germans put in their gardens." Lefrère, 1186. Paterne Berrichon (real name: Pierre Dufour) wrote to Vitalie Rimbaud asking for her daughter's hand in marriage before he had even met Isabelle. He saw that with Isabelle he would acquire joint rights to all the writings of her brother.

7. Yves Reboul, "Les Problèmes rimbaldiens traditionnels et le témoignage d'Isabelle Rimbaud," *La Revue des lettres modernes,* 445–49 (1976): 86.

8. Charles Baudelaire, *Oeuvres,* I: 113.

9. Mircea Eliade comments on rites of initiation as practiced, for instance, in Africa. After the rigors of initiation (solitude, scarification, burns, thirst, and hunger), the catechumen meets his "tutelary spirit," who introduces him to the spiritual realm. Mircea Eliade, *Birth and Rebirth,* 67.

10. Nicholl, 310.

Bibliography

Works by Rimbaud

Rimbaud, Arthur. 2000. *Oeuvres.* Paris: Classiques Garnier. Ed. S. Bernard and A. Guyaux.
———. 1986. *Oeuvres poétiques.* Paris: Imp. nationale. Textes présentés et commentés par C.A. Hackett.
———. 1972. *Oeuvres complètes.* Bibliothèque de la Pléiade. Ed. Antoine Adam. Paris: Gallimard.
———. 1929. *Oeuvres d'Arthur Rimbaud: Vers et proses.* Paris: Mercure de France. Préface de Paul Claudel. Ed. Paterne Berrichon.

Works on Rimbaud

Baudry, J.-L. 1968. "Le Texte de Rimbaud." *Tel Quel* 35: 46–63.
———. 1969. "Le Texte de Rimbaud." *Tel Quel* 36: 33–53.
Bersani, Leo. 1976. *A Future for Astyanax: Character and Desire in Literature.* Boston: Little Brown.
Bonnefoy, Yves. 1994. *Rimbaud.* Paris: Seuil.
———. 1989. *The Act and the Place of Poetry: Selected Essays,* Ed. John T. Naughton. Chicago: University of Chicago Press.
Briet, Suzanne. 1968. *Madame Rimbaud: essai de biographie, suivi de la correspondance de Vitalie Cuif-Rimbaud dont treize lettres inédites.* Paris: Lettres modernes. Minard.
Brunel, Pierre. 1983. *Arthur Rimbaud ou L'éclatant désastre.* Paris: Champ Vallon.

Chambers, Ross. 1968. "'Memoire' de Rimbaud: Essai de lecture." *Essays in French Literature*. University of Nedlands, Western Australia. Vol. 5: 22–37.
Collot, Michel. 1988. *L'Horizon fabuleux*. Vol. 1. Paris: J. Corti.
Delahaye, Ernest. 1923. *Rimbaud: l'Artiste et l'être moral*. Paris: A. Messein.
Guyaux, André. 1985. *Poétique du fragment: Essai sur les 'Illuminations' de Rimbaud*. Neuchâtel: A la Baconnière.
Hackett, Cecil Arthur. 1948. *Rimbaud l'enfant*. Paris: J. Corti.
Heidegger, Martin. "Reply to an inquiry by Roger Munier on the topic 'Aujourd'hui Rimbaud/Rimbaud Today.'" *Archives des Lettres Modernes* No. 160 (1976): 12–17.
Henry, Albert. 1998. *Contributions à la lecture de Rimbaud*. Bruxelles: Académie royale de Belgique.
Johnson, Barbara. 1973. "La Vérité tue: une lecture de 'Conte.'" *Littérature* 11 (October): 68–77.
Kittang, Atle. 1975. *Discours et jeu: Essai d'analyse des textes d'Arthur Rimbaud*. Contributions norvégiennes aux études romanes, no. 5. Bergen: University of Bergen.
Lawler, James. 1992. *Rimbaud's Theatre of the Self*. Cambridge, MA: Harvard University Press.
Lefrère, Jean-Jacques. 2007. *Arthur Rimbaud: Correspondance*. Paris: Fayard.
_____. 2001. *Arthur Rimbaud*. Paris: Fayard.
Minahen, Charles D. 1985. "Tourbillons de lumiere: The Symbolism of Rimbaud's Illuminating Vortices." *Stanford French Review* 9 (3): 351–64.
_____. 1992. *Vortex/t: The Poetics of Turbulence*. University Park: Pennsylvania State University Press.
Munier, Roger. 1976. *Aujourd'hui, Rimbaud . . . : Enquête*. Paris: Lettres modernes.
Nicholl, Charles. 1999. *Somebody Else: Arthur Rimbaud in Africa, 1880–91*. Chicago: University of Chicago Press.
Perloff, Marjorie. 1983. *The Poetics of Indeterminacy: Rimbaud to Cage*. Evanston, IL: Northwestern University Press.
Petitfils, Pierre. 1987. *Rimbaud*. Trans. Alan Sheridan. Charlottesville: University Press of Virginia. Original French edition 1982.
Reboul, Yves. 1976. *Les Problèmes rimbaldiens traditionnels et le témoignage d'Isabelle Rimbaud*. Paris: *La Revue Des Lettres Modernes* 445–449 (1976): 83–102.
Richard, Jean-Pierre. 1955. *Poésie et profondeur*. Paris: Éditions du Seuil.
Robb, Graham. 2000. *Rimbaud*. New York: W.W. Norton.
Ross, Kristin. 1988. *The Emergence of Social Space: Rimbaud and the Paris Commune*. Minneapolis: University of Minnesota Press.
Sacchi, Sergio. 2002. *Etudes sur 'les Illuminations' de Rimbaud*. Paris: Presses de l'Université de Paris–Sorbonne.
Starkie, Enid. 1961. *Arthur Rimbaud*. New York: New Directions.
Steiner, George. 1989. *Real Presences*. Chicago: University of Chicago Press.
Steinmetz, Jean-Luc. 1972. "*Ici, maintenant*, Les Illuminations." *Littérature* 11 (1972): 22–45.

———. 1982. "Exercice de mémoire." *Revue de l'Université de Bruxelles* 1–2: 47–60.
Verlaine, Paul. 1972. *Oeuvres en prose complètes*. Bibliothèque de la Pléiade. Paris: Gallimard.

Psychoanalytic Theory

Bersani, Leo. 1990. *The Culture of Redemption*. Cambridge, MA: Harvard University Press.
Dufresne, Todd. 2007. *Against Freud: Critics Talk Back*. Stanford, CA: Stanford University Press.
Eidelberg, Ludwig, ed. 1968. *Encyclopedia of Psychoanalysis*. New York: Free Press.
Ellison, David. 2001. *Ethics and Aesthetics in Modernist Literature: From the Sublime to the Uncanny*. Cambridge: Cambridge University Press.
Fenichel, Otto. 1945. *The Psychoanalytic Theory of Neurosis*. New York: W.W. Norton & Co.
Freud, Sigmund. 2003. *The Uncanny*. Trans. David McLintock. New York: Penguin Books.
———. 1989. *The Freud Reader*. New York: W.W. Norton.
———. 1965. *New Introductory Lectures on Psychoanalysis*. New York: Norton.
———. 1957. *The Standard Edition of the Complete Psychological Works of Sigmund Freud*. London: Hogarth Press.
Hertz, Neil. 1985. *The End of the Line: Essays on Psychoanalysis and the Sublime*. New York: Columbia University Press.
Klein, Melanie. 1975. "The Early Development of Conscience in the Child." In *Love, Guilt and Reparation and Other Works, 1921–1945*. Vol. 1. New York: Macmillan, The Free Press. First published 1933.
Lagache, Daniel. 1960. "Situation de l'aggressivité." In *Oeuvres IV*. Ed. Eva Rosenblum. Paris: Presses Universitaires de France.
Lagache, Daniel. 1982. "Structure de la personnalité." In *Oeuvres IV*. Ed. Eva Rosenblum. Paris: Presses Universitaires de France.
Laplanche, Jean, and J. B. Pontalis. 1973. *The Language of Psycho-analysis*. Trans. Donald Nicholson-Smith. New York: Norton.
Loewald, Hans. 1988. *Sublimation: Inquiries into Theoretical Psychoanalysis*. New Haven: Yale University Press.
McCall, Raymond. 1983. *Phenomenological Psychology: An Introduction: With a Glossary of Some Key Heideggerian Terms*. Madison: University of Wisconsin Press.
Mitchell, Stephen, and Margaret J. Black. 1995. *Freud and Beyond: A History of Modern Psychoanalytic Thought*. New York: BasicBooks.
Searl, N. 1929. "The Flight to Reality." *International Journal of Psycho-Analysis* 10: 280–91.
Socarides, Charles. 1968. *The Overt Homosexual*. New York: Grune Stratton.
Winnicott, D. W. 1992. *Psycho-analytic Explorations*. Edited by Clare Winnicott,

Ray Shepherd, and Madeleine Davis. Cambridge, MA: Harvard University Press.
Wright, Elizabeth. 1984. *Psychoanalytic Criticism: Theory in Practice*. London, New York: Methuen.

Heidegger

Dreyfus, Hubert L. 2005. "Heidegger's Ontology of Art." In *A Companion to Heidegger*. Ed. H. Dreyfus and M. Wrathall. Oxford: Blackwell Publishing Ltd.
Fóti, Véronique. 1992. *Heidegger and the Poets: Poiesis Sophia Techne*. New Jersey: Humanities Press International.
Guignon, Charles, ed. 1993. *The Cambridge Companion to Heidegger*. Cambridge: Cambridge University Press.
Heidegger, Martin. 2002. *Off the Beaten Track*. Trans. J. Young and K. Haynes. Cambridge: Cambridge University Press.
———. 1975. *Poetry, Language, Thought*. Trans. Albert Hofstadter. New York: HarperCollins.
———. 1962. *Being and Time*. Trans. John MacQuarrie and Edward Robinson. New York: Harper Row.
Hölderlin, Friedrich. 1967. *Poems and Fragments*. Trans. Michael Hamburger. Ann Arbor: University of Michigan Press.
Taylor, Charles. 1992. "Heidegger, Language, and Ecology." In *Heidegger: A Critical Reader*. Eds. Hubert Dreyfus and Harrison Hall. Oxford: Cambridge University Press.

Other Writers

Barthes, Roland. 1973. *Le plaisir du texte*. Paris: Seuil.
Baudelaire, Charles. 1944. "Le Génie enfant." In *Oeuvres*. Bibliothèque de la Pléiade ed. Vol. 1. Paris: Gallimard.
Claudel, François. 2006. "Rimbaud chez Claudel ou une visite à Brangues." *Rimbaud Vivant* 45: 117.
Eliade, Mircea. 1958. *Birth and Rebirth: The Religious Meanings of Initiation in Human Culture*. New York: Harper.
Hemmings, F. 1982. *Baudelaire the Damned: A Biography*. New York: Scribner.
Lanham, Richard. 1991. *A Handlist of Rhetorical Terms*. Berkeley: University of California Press.
Mason, Edward. 1967. *The Paris Commune: An Episode in the History of the Socialist Movement*. New York: Fertig.
Michelet, Jules. 1964. *La Sorcière*. Paris: Julliard.
———. 1858. *L'Amour*. Paris: Flammarion.
Mitzman, Arthur. 1990. *Michelet, Historian: Rebirth and Romanticism in Nineteenth-Century France*. New Haven: Yale University Press.

Peyre, Henri. 1962. *Baudelaire, a Collection of Critical Essays*. Englewood Cliffs, NJ: Prentice-Hall.
Pineau, Joseph. 1979. *Le Mouvement rythmique en français*. Paris: Klincksieck.
Quinet, Edgar. 1842. *La Génie des religions*. Paris: Librairie Hachette.
Scott, Clive. 1986. *A Question of Syllables: Essays in Nineteenth-century French Verse*. Cambridge: Cambridge University Press.
Valéry, Paul. 1957. *Cahiers*. Paris: Centre national de la recherche scientifique.

Index

Adam, Antoine, 46, 54, 79
L'Africain, R's uncle, his first contact with "the dark continent," 127

Balzac, Honoré de, 79
Bardey, Alfred, R's employer in Harar, 147–48
Barthes, Roland, 2, 111, 116
Baudelaire, Charles, 1, 5, 11, 27–29, 75, 82–84, 116, 124, 145, 146, 157–58n9 (chap. 15)
Baudry, J.-L., 1
Bernard, Suzanne, 7, 55, 69, 70, 71, 90, 107
Berrichon, Paterne, 143, 145
Bersani, Leo, 12–13, 34, 86, 121, 122–23, 129, 153n5 (chap. 7), 154n2 (chap. 10)
Bonnefoy, Yves, 4, 11–12, 20–21, 23, 39, 62, 64, 73, 95, 107, 114–15, 121
Bretagne, Charles, 26
Briet, Suzanne, 36, 37
Brunel, P., 12

Carjat, Étienne, made famous photos of R, was attacked by R at meeting of Les Vilains Bonshommes/ The Nasty Goodfellows, 154n1 (chap. 8)
Chambers, Ross, 33–34
Char, René, 97
Chateaubriand, François-René de, 79
Chaulier, Canon A., chaplain at Conception Hospital in Marseilles, where R. died, 6, 108, 145, 146–47
Claudel, Paul, 62, 102, 133, 136, 143, 145
Cloutier, Mme, R's wet-nurse, 1, 90
Cocteau, Jean, 91
Collot, Michel, 13, 36, 150–51n19

Delahaye, Ernest, R's boyhood friend, 25, 38, 43, 44, 46, 72, 120, 156n6 (chap. 13)
Demeny, Paul, one of the two recipients of "la lettre du voyant," 25, 104

Dreyfus, Herbert L., 21
Dufresne, Todd, 149n4
Ellison, David, 149n6, 151n1 (chap. 3)

Empedocles, 47, 48–49
Empson, William, 111

Fantin-Latour, Ignace-Henri, painted picture of R and Les Vilains Bonshommes, 153
Fenichel, Otto, 105
Flack, Roberta, singer of soulful jazz and pop ballads, 154
Forain, Jean-Louis, known as Gavroche, "le gamin de Paris," after a character in Hugo's Les Misérables, xi
Fóti, Véronique, 156n2 (chap. 13)
Fowlie, Wallace, 97, 141–42
Freud, Sigmund, 2, 3, 5, 12, 25, 27–28, 59, 65–66, 76, 79, 89, 95–96, 129–30, 146

Genet, Jean, 84, 86
Godchot, Colonel, 43
Guignon, Charles, 122
Guyaux, André, 6, 7, 14, 46, 53, 55, 80, 82, 86, 107–8, 121

Hackett, Cecil Arthur, 11, 12, 13, 14, 16, 36
Harrison, Jim, poet and novelist, 103
Heidegger, Martin, 3, 6, 13, 23, 32, 101, 104, 111–13, 115, 116, 137, 139, 148, 231
Henry, Albert, 60
Hertz, Neil, 30
Hölderlin, Friedrich, 150n12
Hugo, Victor, 25, 26–27
Husserl, Edmund, 13

Imperial Prince, son of Emperor Louis-Napoléon and Empress Eugénie, 154n2 (chap. 9)
Izambard, Georges, R's teacher at the College of Charleville and the second recipient of "la lettre du voyant," 25, 43, 46, 70, 85, 104, 145

Johnson, Barbara, 82, 84

Kittang, Atle, 33
Klein, Melanie, 5, 12, 14, 35, 48, 61, 62, 89, 90

Lagache, Daniel, 12, 87, 97
Laplanche, Jean-Jacques, 39, 146
Lawler, James, 27, 33, 62, 68, 70, 82, 83, 86, 87, 97, 124, 131, 133, 157n3 (chap. 15)
Lefrère, Jean-Jacques, 26, 43, 44, 143, 144
Loewald, Hans, 14–15, 122, 123

Mallarmé, Stéphane, 49, 77, 84
Mason, Edward, 44, 51
Mauté, Mathilde, Verlaine's wife, 119–20, 129
Matucci, Mario, 133
Mauriac, François, 143
Mauron, Charles, 2
Michelet, Jules, 25, 64, 71, 95, 124, 126
Minahen, Charles D., 49
Mitchell, Stephen, 89
Mitzman, Arthur, 155n1 (chap. 12)

Nicholl, Charles, 144, 147–48
Nietzsche, Friedrich, 4–5, 21, 107
Nouveau, Germain, 78, 122

Pascal, Blaise, 2, 135
Perloff, Marjorie, 6, 111–12
Petitfils, Pierre, 44, 120, 158n12
Pineau, Joseph, 90
Plato, 74
Pontalis, J. B., 39
Proust, Marcel, 12, 23, 122–23

Quinet, Edgar, 25, 95, 101, 126

Reboul, Yves, 145
Richard, Jean-Pierre, 149n3

Rimbaud, Arthur, poems and collections by:
  A Une Raison, 5, 51–54
  Adieu, 15–16, 137–40
  Angoisse, 3, 5, 68–72, 144
  Après le déluge, 5, 59, 85
  Au Cabaret-Vert, 21, 90
  Aube, 5, 72–74, 137
  Barbare, 14, 137
  Le Bateau ivre, 2, 4, 5, 24–32, 72, 89, 116, 137, 138, 147
  Chant de guerre parisien, 44, 60
  Conte, 5, 74, 82–87, 90
  Le Coeur du pitre, 45–46, 81, 85
  Délires I, 130–31
  Délires II, 131
  Démocratie, 5, 54–56
  L'Éternite, 29
  L'Éclair, 133–35
  Génie, 6, 95–102, 103
  H, 5, 80–81, 84
  Honte, 5, 12, 65–68, 119
  Illuminations, 6, 7, 12, 20, 34, 51, 75, 108, 111, 113, 115, 145
  L'Impossible, 131–33
  La Lettre du voyant, 6, 13, 115
  Ma Bohême, 21
  Le mal, 60
  Matin, 135–37
  Mauvais sang, 125–28
  Mémoire, 4, 5, 14, 15, 29, 33–40, 50
  Nocturne vulgaire, 5, 88–91, 137
  Nuit de l'enfer, 128–30
  Ophélie, 33, 35
  Les Poètes de sept ans, 4, 19–23, 114–15
  Qu'est-ce pour nous, mon coeur . . . ?, 47–50, 60
  Une Saison en enfer, 6, 15, 53, 54–56, 77, 79, 116, 118, 119–40, 144
  Solde, 6, 103–8
  Soleil et chair, 21
  Vagabonds, 106
  Vie I, 75–77, 79
  Vie II, 77–79
  Vie III, 79–80
  Villes II, 6, 111–18
Rimbaud, Frédéric (R's brother), 1, 36, 38
Rimbaud, Frédéric (R's father), 1, 4, 36, 39–40, 48–50, 96
Rimbaud, Isabelle (R's sister), 1–2, 6, 108, 142–44, 147
Rimbaud, Marie-Catherine-Vitalie Cuif (R's mother), 1–2, 4, 11–12, 14, 19–20, 22–23, 30, 36, 37, 39, 43–44, 49, 55, 79, 90, 96, 114, 115, 117–18, 125, 129, 134–35, 137, 142
Rimbaud, Vitalie (R's sister), 1, 35
Rivière, Jacques, 75, 90
Robb, Graham, 12, 87
Ronsard, Pierre de, 77
Ross, Kristin, 55

Sacchi, Sergio, 14, 60, 76, 78
Sartre, Jean-Paul, 86
Schneider, Hortense, one of Offenbach's divas and a notorious courtesan, 80–81, 85, 90
Scott, Clive, 154n5 (chap. 8)
Searl, N., 154n1 (chap. 9)
Socarides, Charles, 39
Spinoza, Baruch, 65
Starkie, Enid, 26, 64, 85, 151n2 (chap. 2)
Steiner, George, 12
Steinmetz, Jean-Luc, 14

Todorov, Tzvetan, 112

Valéry, Paul, 121, 133
Verlaine, Paul, 6, 13, 14, 26, 28, 62, 65, 78, 85, 119–23, 125, 126, 129, 137

Winnicott, D. W., 5, 14, 19–20, 47–48, 50, 127
Wright, Elizabeth, 11

Zola, Émile, 80

www.ingramcontent.com/pod-product-compliance
Lightning Source LLC
Chambersburg PA
CBHW020802160426
43192CB00006B/414